VOLUME TWO: THE SPAWN OF DRACULA

THE CHRONICLES OF
LEGION

SCRIPT
FABIEN
NURY

ART
MARIO
ALBERTI

ZHANG
XIAOYU

TIRSO

TITAN COMICS

THE CHRONICLES OF
LEGION

VOLUME TWO: THE SPAWN OF DRACULA

Collection Editor
Gabriela Houston

Collection Designer
Dan Bura

Senior Editor
Steve White

Titan Comics Editorial
**Andrew James,
Tom Williams**

Production Manager
Obi Onuora

Production Supervisor
Jackie Flook

Production Assistant
Peter James

Studio Manager
Emma Smith

Circulation Manager
Steve Tothill

Marketing Manager
Ricky Claydon

Senior Marketing and Press
Executive
Owen Johnson

Publishing Manager
Darryl Tothill

Publishing Director
Chris Teather

Operations Director
Leigh Baulch

Executive Director
Vivian Cheung

Publisher
Nick Landau

THE STORY SO FAR

Two brothers, Vlad Tepes Dracula and Radu, have achieved immortality by being able to transfer their consciousness between bodies using the power that rests in their blood...

March 1531, The Atlantic: A mysterious beauty, Gabriella Doña de la Fuente, travels to the New World, seeking to marry a famous conquistador, Hernan Cortes, but with a much more sinister plan in mind...

January 1812, Moscow: Captain Armand Malachi recruits mercenaries from Napoleon's army in order to recover a lost, mysterious treasure...

October 1885, London: Victor Douglas Thorpe, a gambler down on his luck, comes into a curious and dramatic inheritance...

The blood of Vlad flows in the veins of all three. Against their knowledge, and their will, this trio will find themselves hurled into an eternal battle between the two vampiric brothers.

WRITTEN BY
FABIEN NURY

ART BY
MARIO ALBERTI
PAGES 15-38

ZHANG XIAOYU
PAGES 41-52

TIRSO
PAGES 3-14, 39-40, 53-56
COLORS BY: JAVIER MARTIN

COVER ART BY
MARIO ALBERTI

TRANSLATED BY
VIRGINIE SELAVY

LETTERING BY
GABRIELA HOUSTON

What did you think of this book?

We love to hear from our readers. Please email us at: readercomments@titanemail.com, or write to us at the above address.

To receive news, competitions, and exclusive offers online, please sign up for the Titan Comics newsletter on our website: **www.titan-comics.com**

Follow us on Twitter **@ComicsTitan**

Visit us at **facebook.com/comicstitan**

The Chronicles of Legion Volume Two: The Spawn Of Dracula
ISBN: 9781782760948

Published by Titan Comics
A division of Titan Publishing Group Ltd.
144 Southwark St. London SE1 0UP

A CIP catalogue record for this title is available from the British Library.
First edition: December 2014
Originally published in 2011 by Éditions Glénat, France as *Les Chroniques de Legion: Livre 2*

10 9 8 7 6 5 4 3 2 1

Printed in China.
Titan Comics.   TC0201

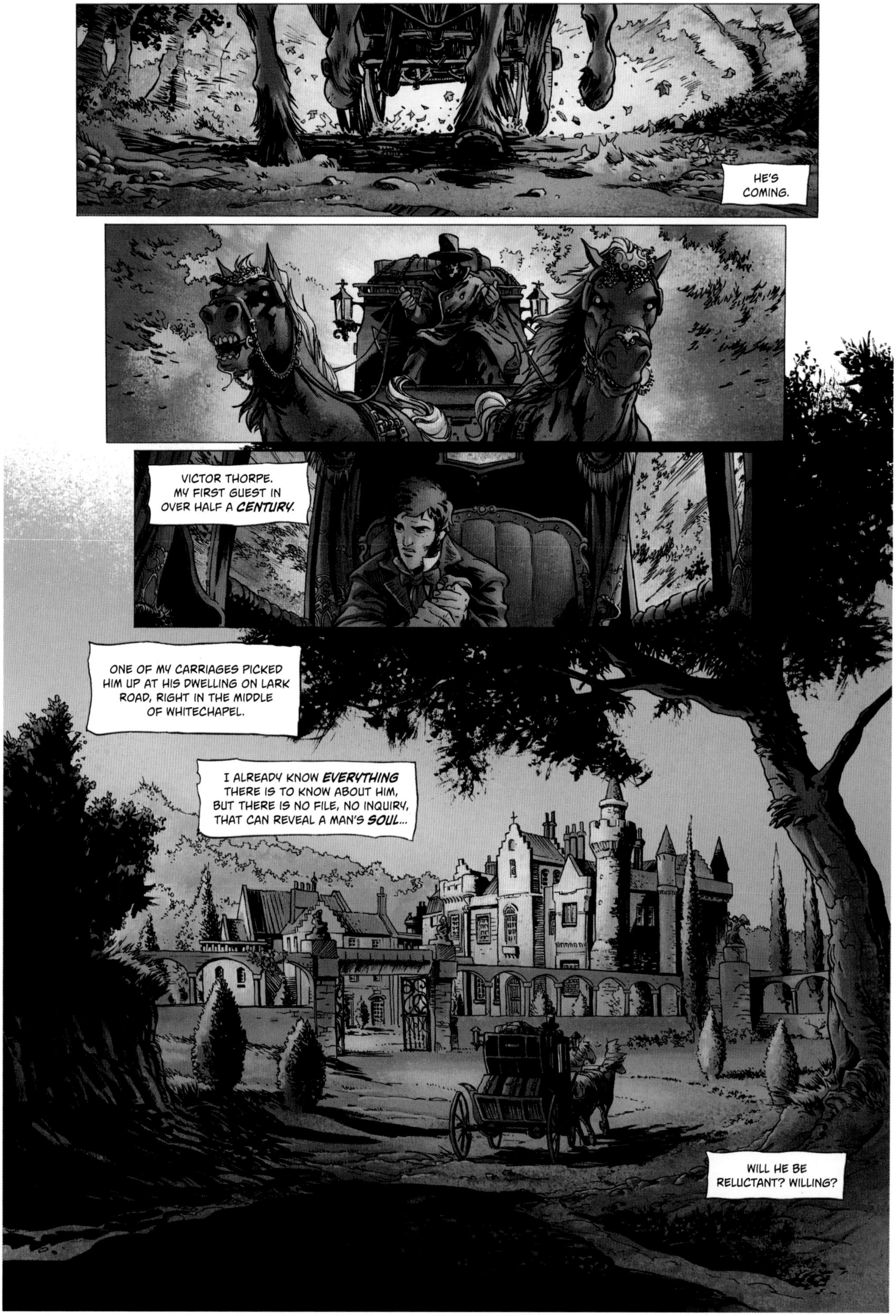
HE'S COMING.
VICTOR THORPE. MY FIRST GUEST IN OVER HALF A CENTURY.
ONE OF MY CARRIAGES PICKED HIM UP AT HIS DWELLING ON LARK ROAD, RIGHT IN THE MIDDLE OF WHITECHAPEL.
I ALREADY KNOW EVERYTHING THERE IS TO KNOW ABOUT HIM, BUT THERE IS NO FILE, NO INQUIRY, THAT CAN REVEAL A MAN'S SOUL...
WILL HE BE RELUCTANT? WILLING?

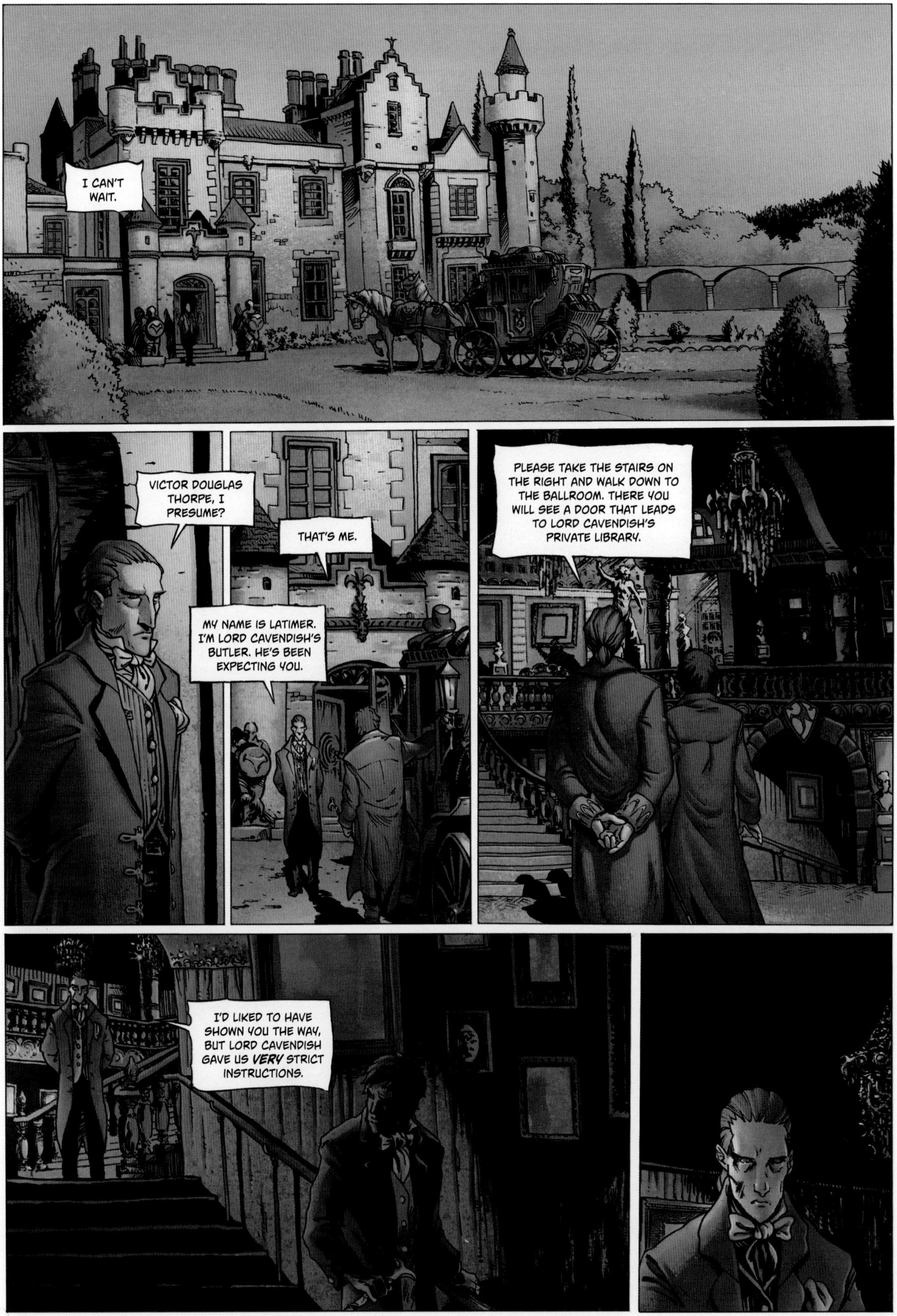
I CAN'T WAIT.
VICTOR DOUGLAS THORPE, I PRESUME?
THAT'S ME.
MY NAME IS LATIMER. I'M LORD CAVENDISH'S BUTLER. HE'S BEEN EXPECTING YOU.
PLEASE TAKE THE STAIRS ON THE RIGHT AND WALK DOWN TO THE BALLROOM. THERE YOU WILL SEE A DOOR THAT LEADS TO LORD CAVENDISH'S PRIVATE LIBRARY.
I'D LIKED TO HAVE SHOWN YOU THE WAY, BUT LORD CAVENDISH GAVE US VERY STRICT INSTRUCTIONS.

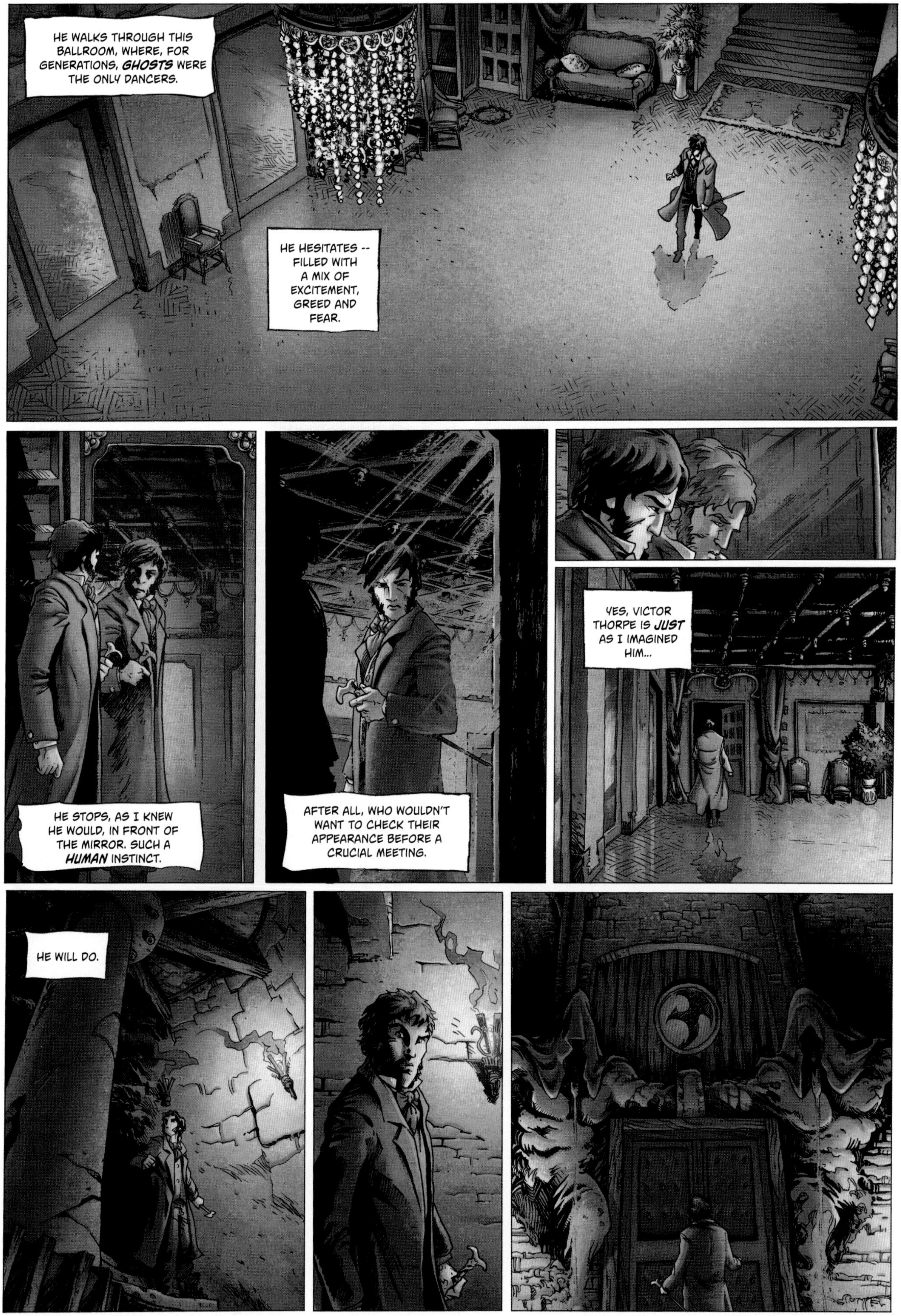
HE WALKS THROUGH THIS BALLROOM, WHERE, FOR GENERATIONS, GHOSTS WERE THE ONLY DANCERS.
HE HESITATES -- FILLED WITH A MIX OF EXCITEMENT, GREED AND FEAR.
HE STOPS, AS I KNEW HE WOULD, IN FRONT OF THE MIRROR. SUCH A HUMAN INSTINCT.
AFTER ALL, WHO WOULDN'T WANT TO CHECK THEIR APPEARANCE BEFORE A CRUCIAL MEETING.
YES, VICTOR THORPE IS JUST AS I IMAGINED HIM...
HE WILL DO.

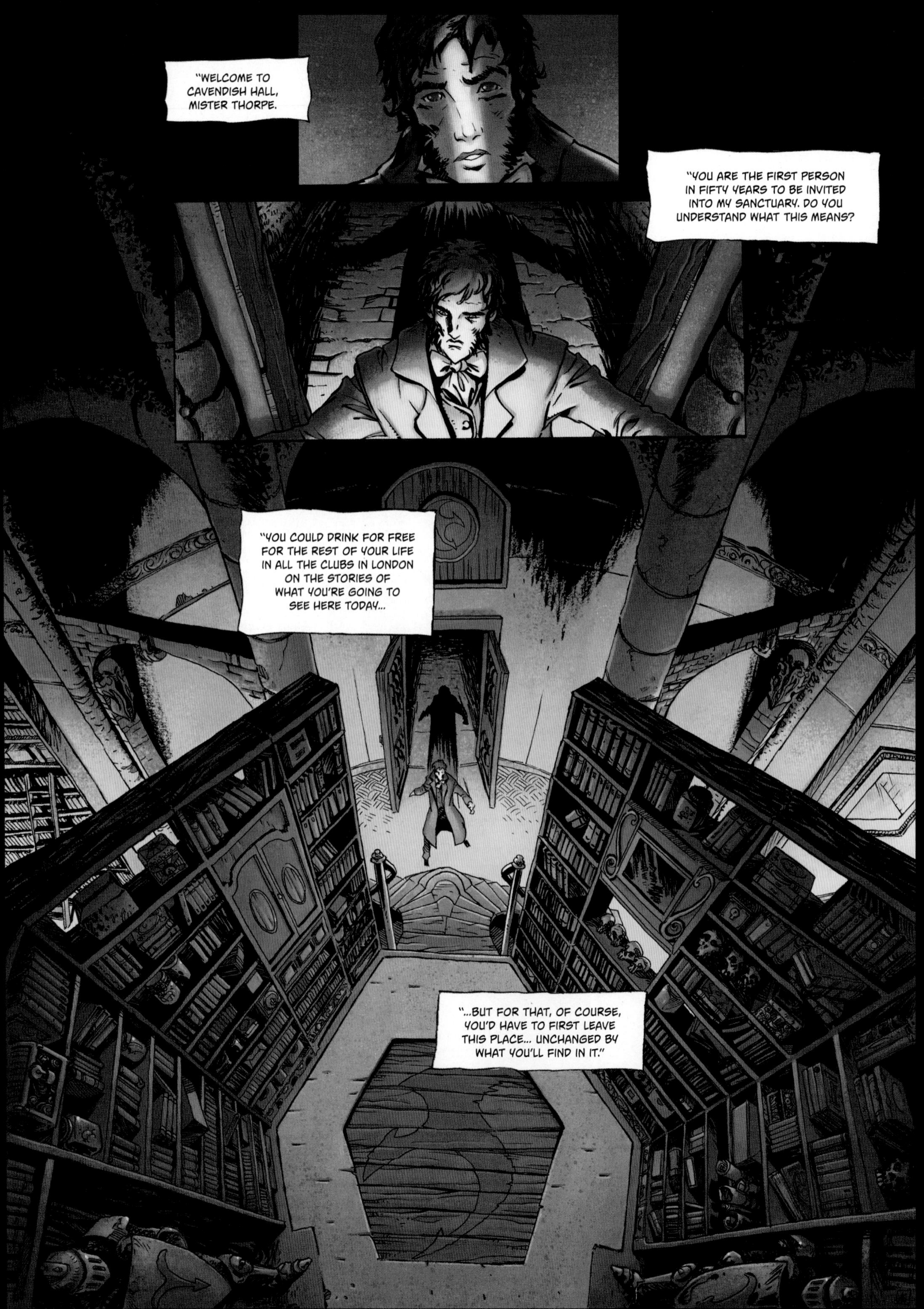
"WELCOME TO CAVENDISH HALL, MISTER THORPE.
"YOU ARE THE FIRST PERSON IN FIFTY YEARS TO BE INVITED INTO MY SANCTUARY. DO YOU UNDERSTAND WHAT THIS MEANS?
"YOU COULD DRINK FOR FREE FOR THE REST OF YOUR LIFE IN ALL THE CLUBS IN LONDON ON THE STORIES OF WHAT YOU'RE GOING TO SEE HERE TODAY...
"...BUT FOR THAT, OF COURSE, YOU'D HAVE TO FIRST LEAVE THIS PLACE... UNCHANGED BY WHAT YOU'LL FIND IN IT."

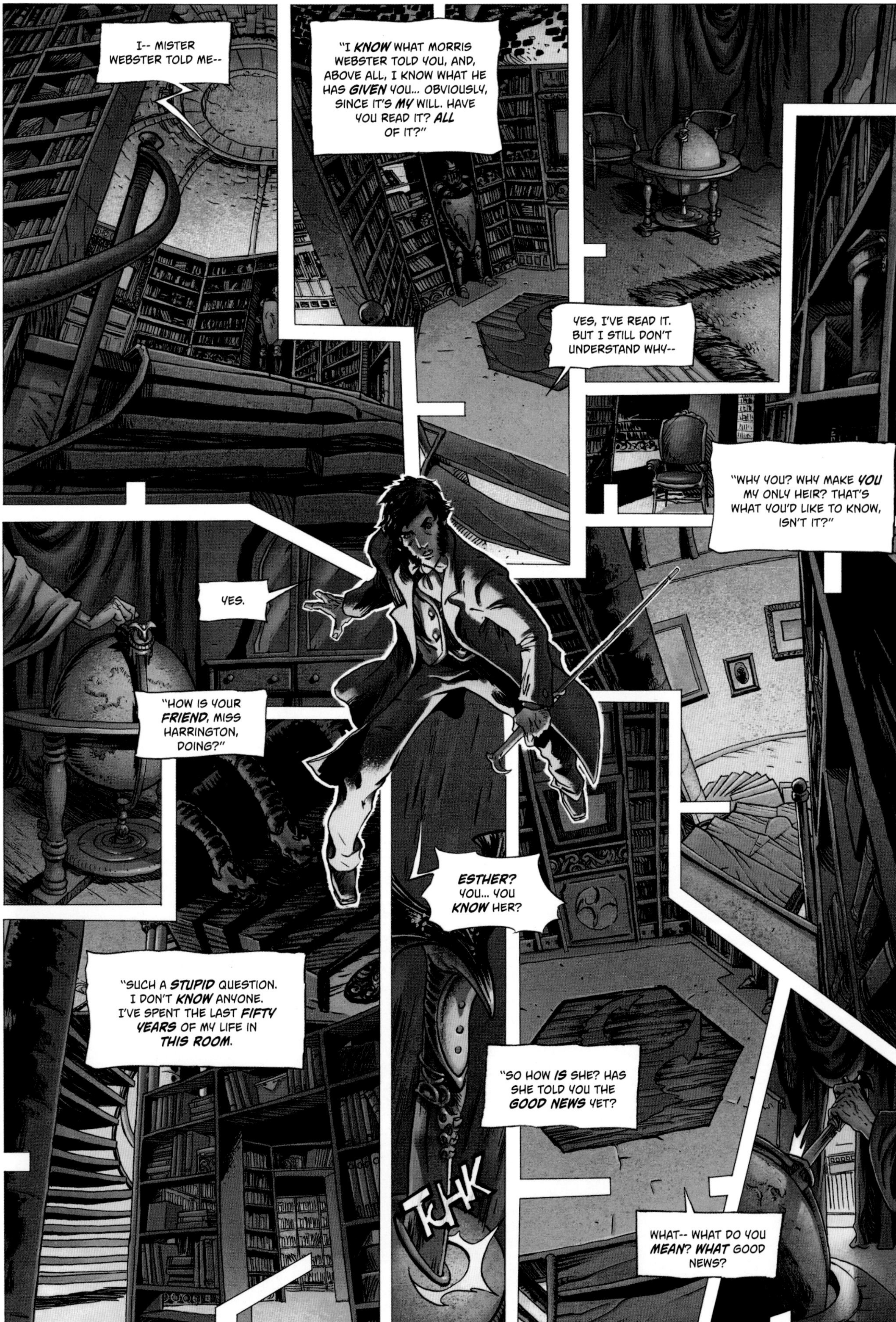
I-- MISTER WEBSTER TOLD ME--
"I KNOW WHAT MORRIS WEBSTER TOLD YOU, AND, ABOVE ALL, I KNOW WHAT HE HAS GIVEN YOU... OBVIOUSLY, SINCE IT'S MY WILL. HAVE YOU READ IT? ALL OF IT?"
YES, I'VE READ IT. BUT I STILL DON'T UNDERSTAND WHY--
"WHY YOU? WHY MAKE YOU MY ONLY HEIR? THAT'S WHAT YOU'D LIKE TO KNOW, ISN'T IT?"
YES.
"HOW IS YOUR FRIEND, MISS HARRINGTON, DOING?"
ESTHER? YOU... YOU KNOW HER?
"SUCH A STUPID QUESTION. I DON'T KNOW ANYONE. I'VE SPENT THE LAST FIFTY YEARS OF MY LIFE IN THIS ROOM.
"SO HOW IS SHE? HAS SHE TOLD YOU THE GOOD NEWS YET?
TCHK
WHAT-- WHAT DO YOU MEAN? WHAT GOOD NEWS?

COME NOW, MISTER THORPE, DON'T PRETEND YOU DON'T **ALREADY** KNOW. HASN'T MISS HARRINGTON PUT ON A LITTLE WEIGHT LATELY? DOES SHE NOT SUFFER FROM A TOUCH OF NAUSEA IN THE MORNINGS?

NO... **NO!** I DON'T **WANT--**

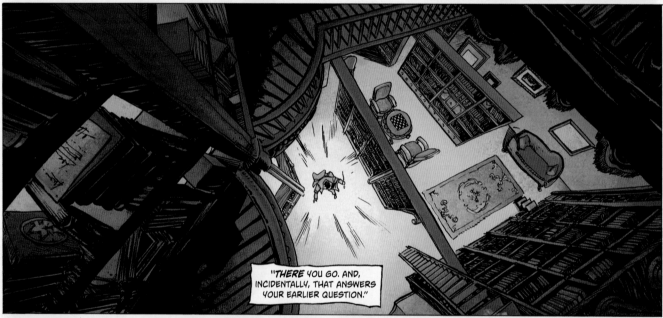

"**THERE** YOU GO. AND, INCIDENTALLY, THAT ANSWERS YOUR EARLIER QUESTION."

I CHOSE YOU BECAUSE YOU ARE **SELFISH**.

GLACK!

OTHER MEN WOULD HAVE ALREADY FACED UP TO THEIR RESPONSIBILITIES, AND LED THEIR BELOVED DOWN THE AISLE...

"...BUT NOT **YOU**."

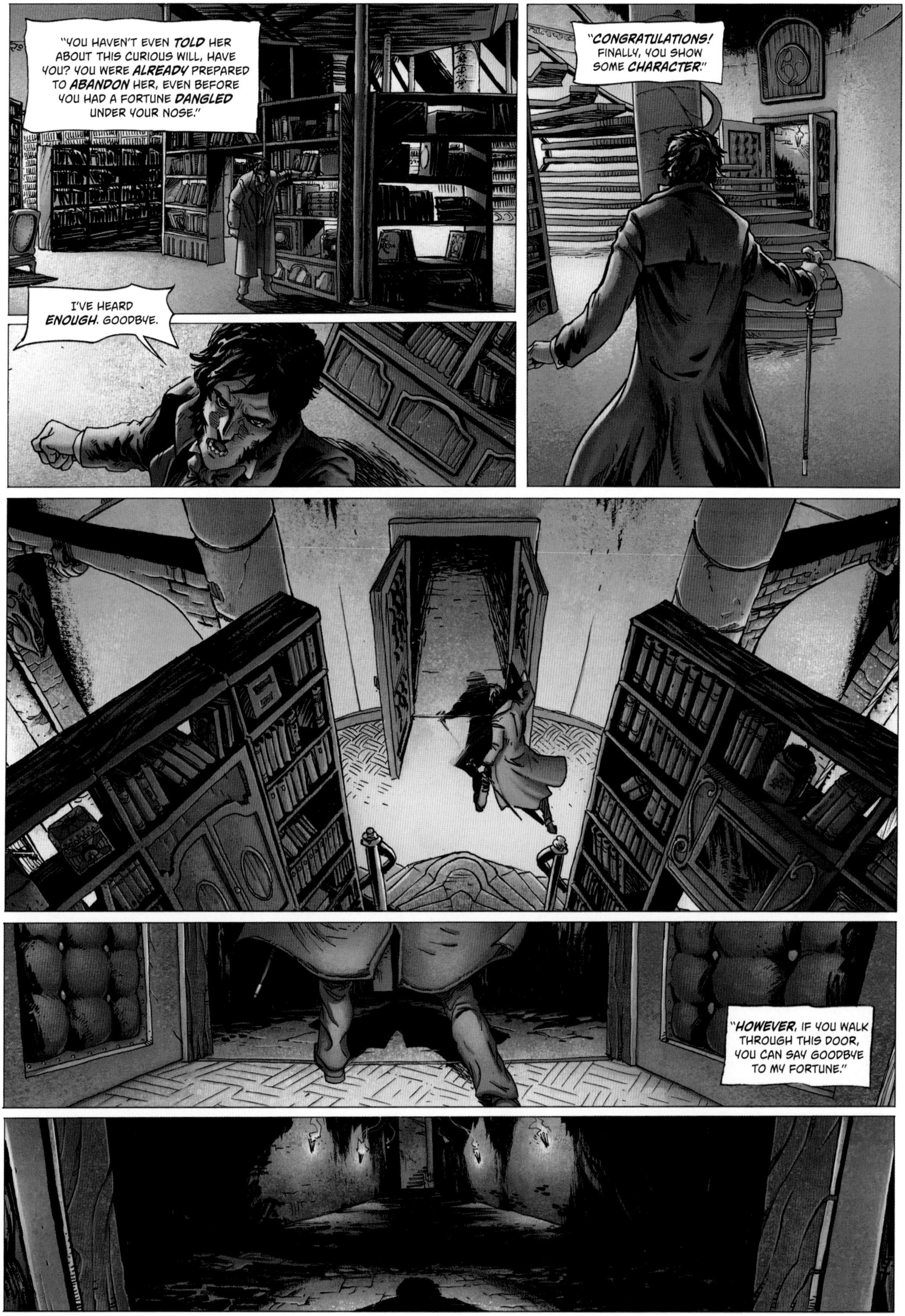
"YOU HAVEN'T EVEN TOLD HER ABOUT THIS CURIOUS WILL, HAVE YOU? YOU WERE ALREADY PREPARED TO ABANDON HER, EVEN BEFORE YOU HAD A FORTUNE DANGLED UNDER YOUR NOSE."
I'VE HEARD ENOUGH. GOODBYE.
"CONGRATULATIONS! FINALLY, YOU SHOW SOME CHARACTER."
"HOWEVER, IF YOU WALK THROUGH THIS DOOR, YOU CAN SAY GOODBYE TO MY FORTUNE."

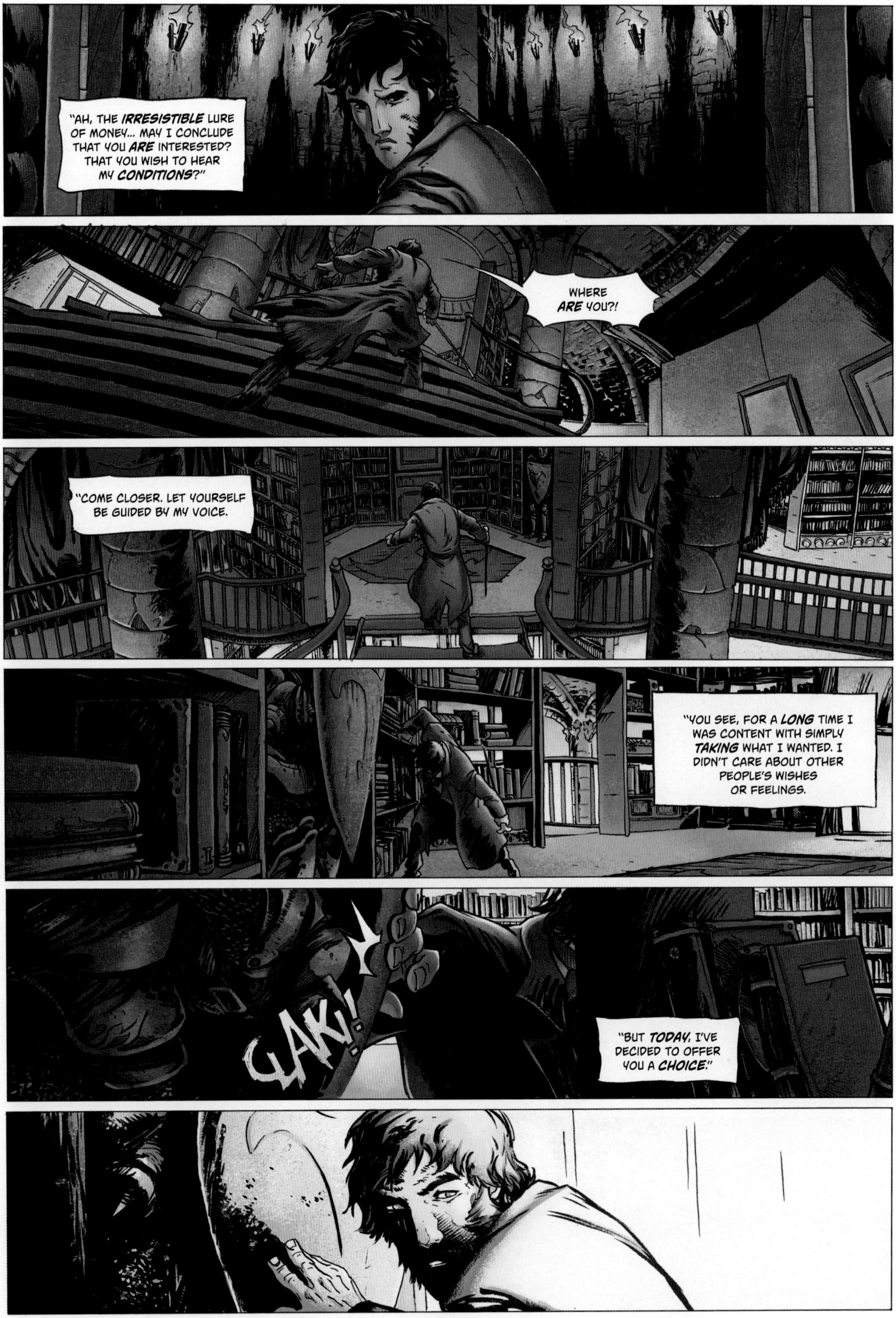
"AH, THE IRRESISTIBLE LURE OF MONEY... MAY I CONCLUDE THAT YOU ARE INTERESTED? THAT YOU WISH TO HEAR MY CONDITIONS?"
WHERE ARE YOU?!
"COME CLOSER. LET YOURSELF BE GUIDED BY MY VOICE.
"YOU SEE, FOR A LONG TIME I WAS CONTENT WITH SIMPLY TAKING WHAT I WANTED. I DIDN'T CARE ABOUT OTHER PEOPLE'S WISHES OR FEELINGS.
GAK!
"BUT TODAY, I'VE DECIDED TO OFFER YOU A CHOICE."

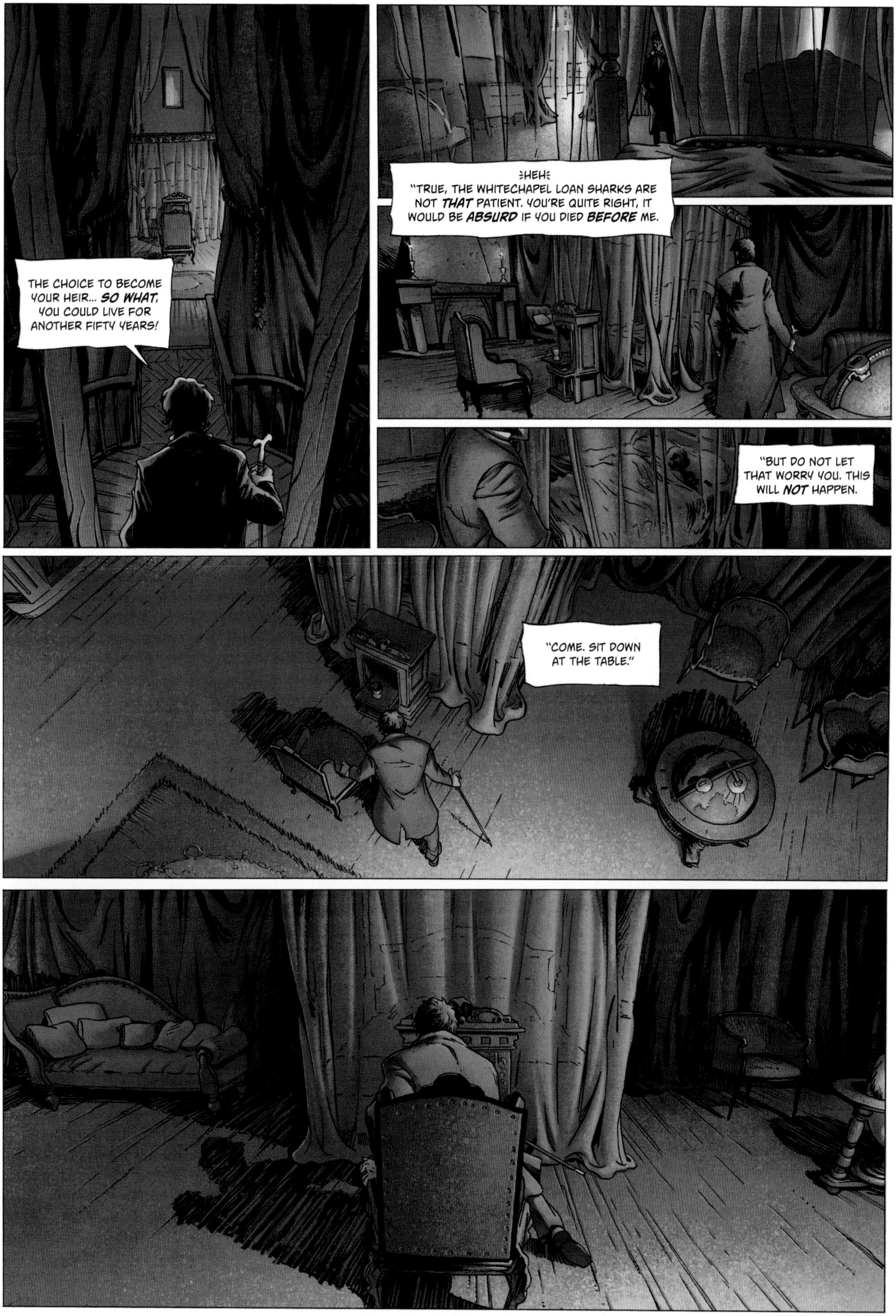
THE CHOICE TO BECOME YOUR HEIR... **SO WHAT,** YOU COULD LIVE FOR ANOTHER FIFTY YEARS!
HEH
"TRUE, THE WHITECHAPEL LOAN SHARKS ARE NOT ***THAT*** PATIENT. YOU'RE QUITE RIGHT, IT WOULD BE ***ABSURD*** IF YOU DIED ***BEFORE*** ME.
"BUT DO NOT LET THAT WORRY YOU. THIS WILL ***NOT*** HAPPEN.
"COME. SIT DOWN AT THE TABLE."

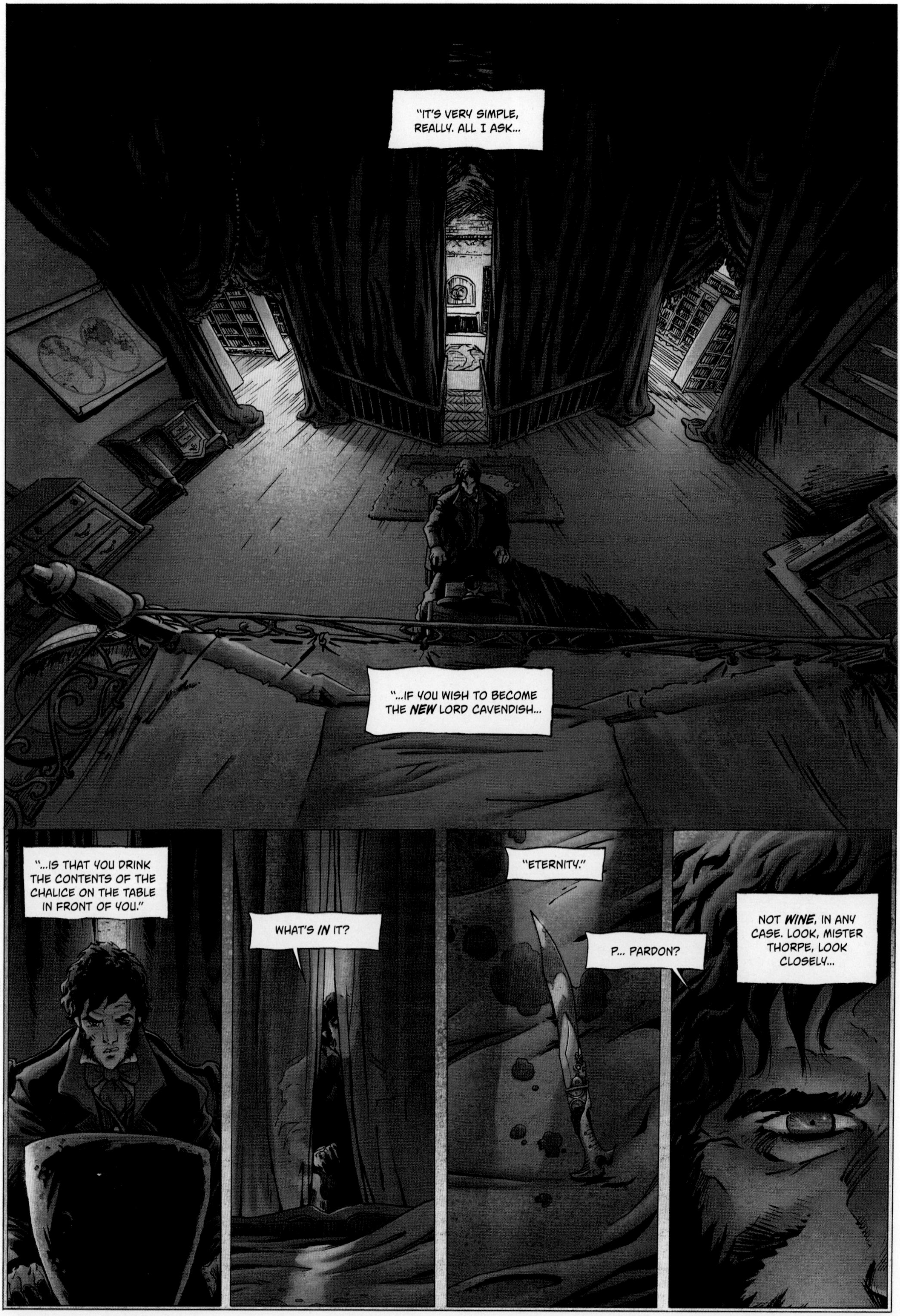
"IT'S VERY SIMPLE, REALLY. ALL I ASK...
"...IF YOU WISH TO BECOME THE NEW LORD CAVENDISH...
"...IS THAT YOU DRINK THE CONTENTS OF THE CHALICE ON THE TABLE IN FRONT OF YOU."
WHAT'S IN IT?
"ETERNITY."
P... PARDON?
NOT WINE, IN ANY CASE. LOOK, MISTER THORPE, LOOK CLOSELY...

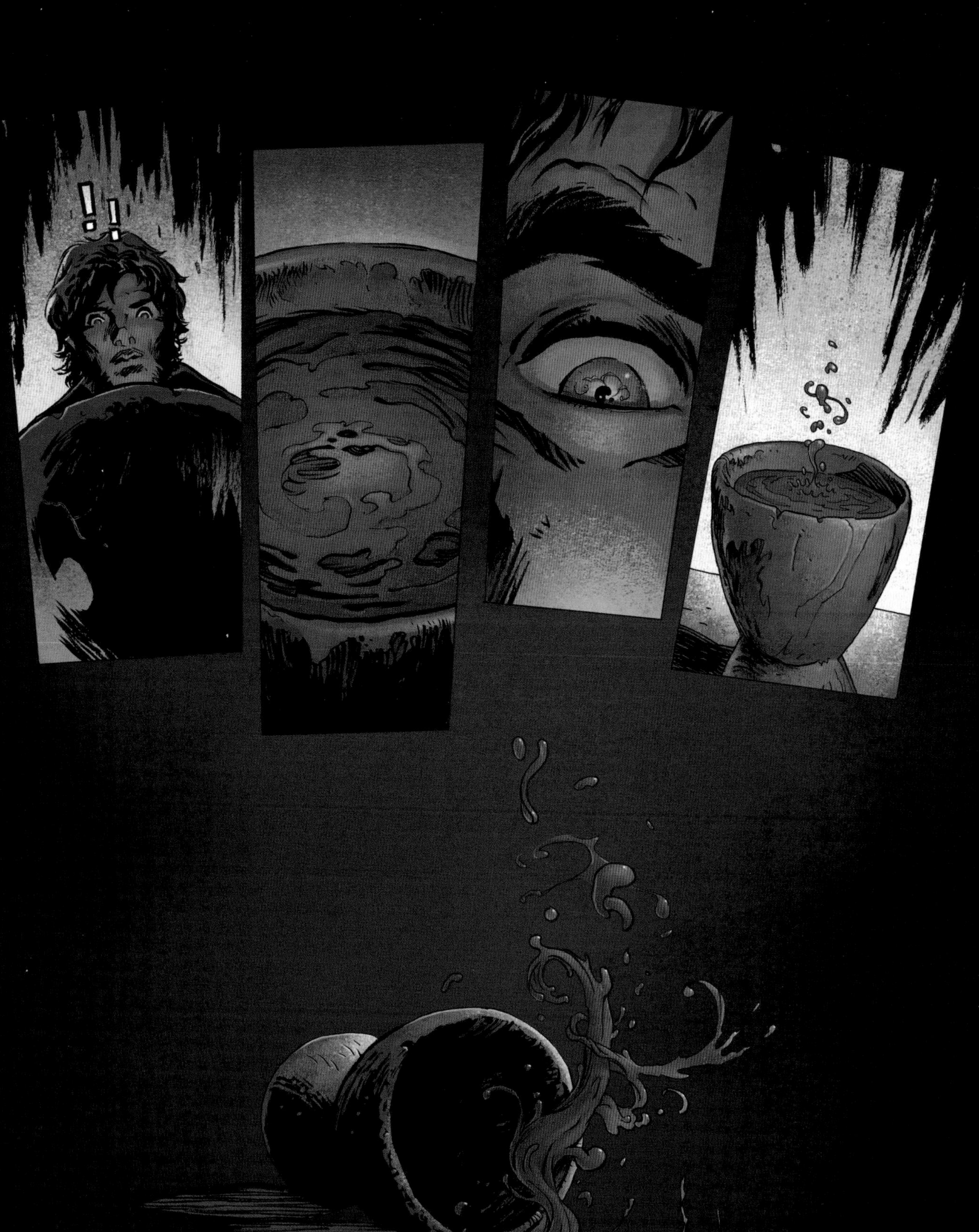
!!

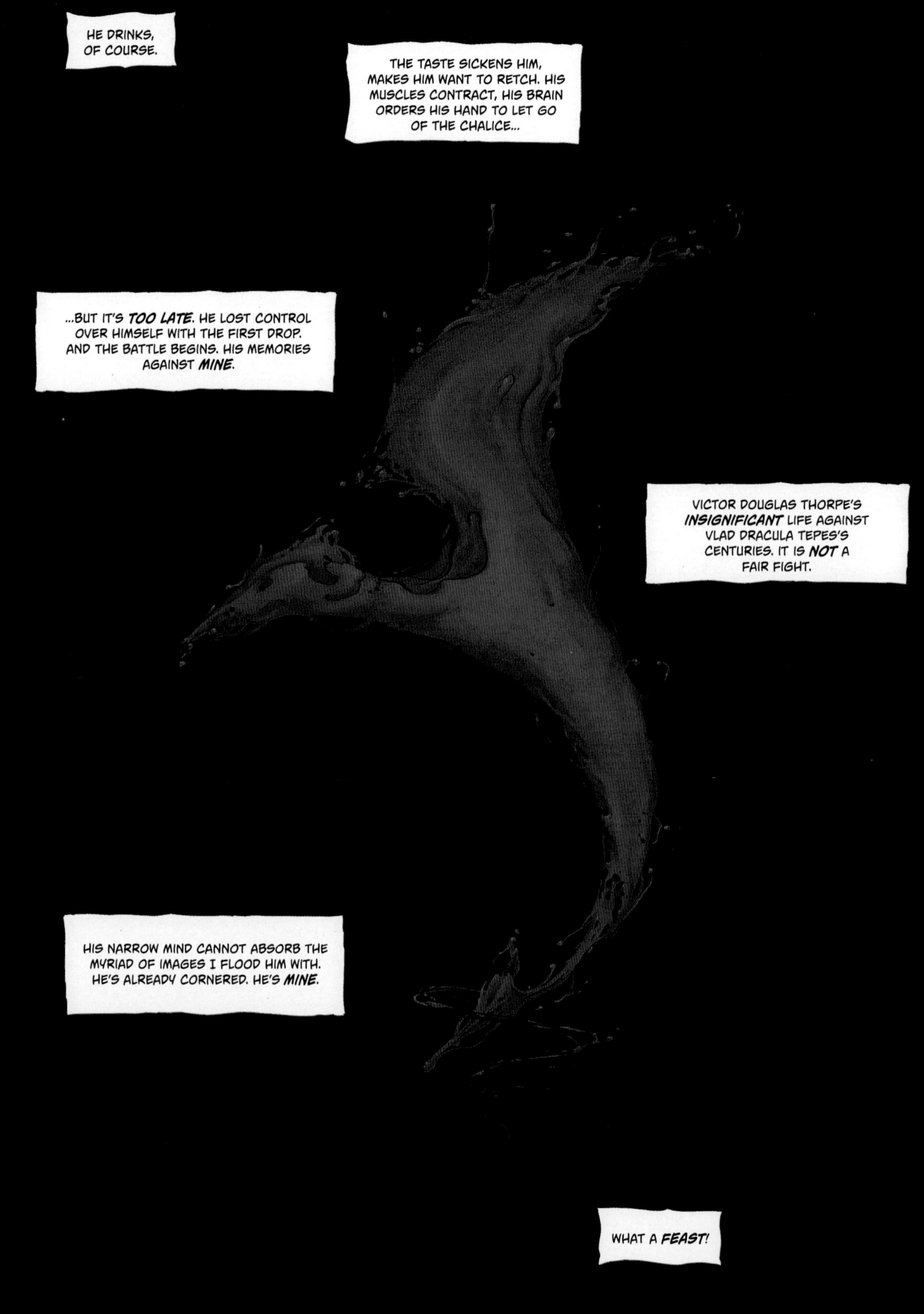
HE DRINKS, OF COURSE.
THE TASTE SICKENS HIM, MAKES HIM WANT TO RETCH. HIS MUSCLES CONTRACT, HIS BRAIN ORDERS HIS HAND TO LET GO OF THE CHALICE...
...BUT IT'S TOO LATE. HE LOST CONTROL OVER HIMSELF WITH THE FIRST DROP. AND THE BATTLE BEGINS. HIS MEMORIES AGAINST MINE.
VICTOR DOUGLAS THORPE'S INSIGNIFICANT LIFE AGAINST VLAD DRACULA TEPES'S CENTURIES. IT IS NOT A FAIR FIGHT.
HIS NARROW MIND CANNOT ABSORB THE MYRIAD OF IMAGES I FLOOD HIM WITH. HE'S ALREADY CORNERED. HE'S MINE.
WHAT A FEAST!

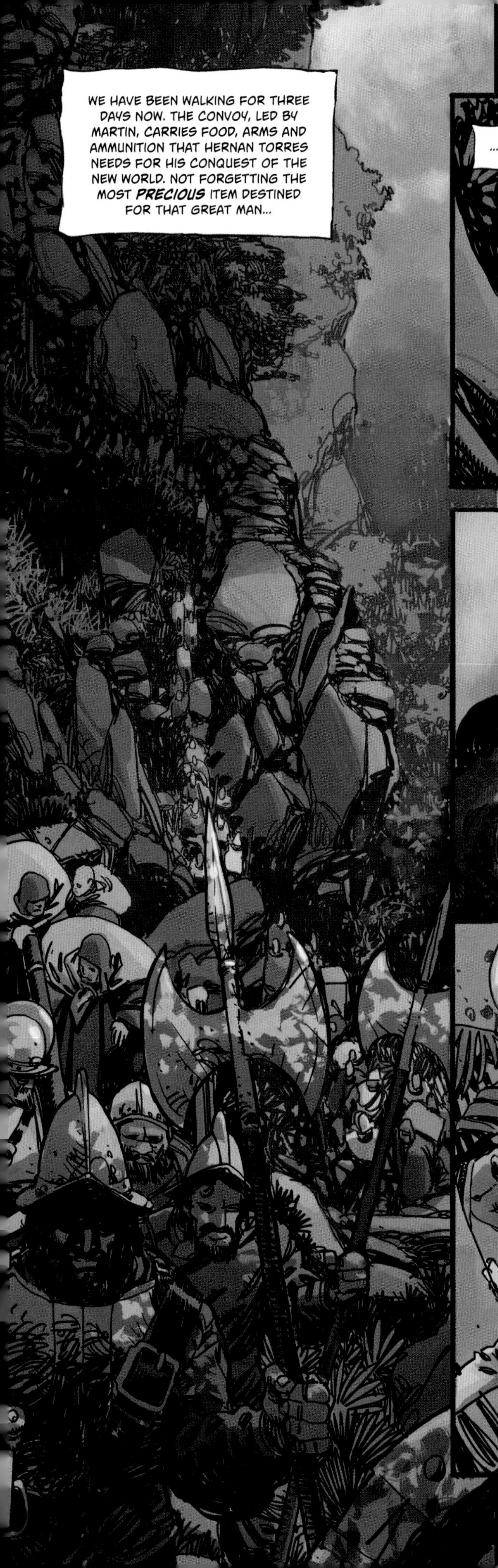
WE HAVE BEEN WALKING FOR THREE DAYS NOW. THE CONVOY, LED BY MARTIN, CARRIES FOOD, ARMS AND AMMUNITION THAT HERNAN TORRES NEEDS FOR HIS CONQUEST OF THE NEW WORLD. NOT FORGETTING THE MOST PRECIOUS ITEM DESTINED FOR THAT GREAT MAN...

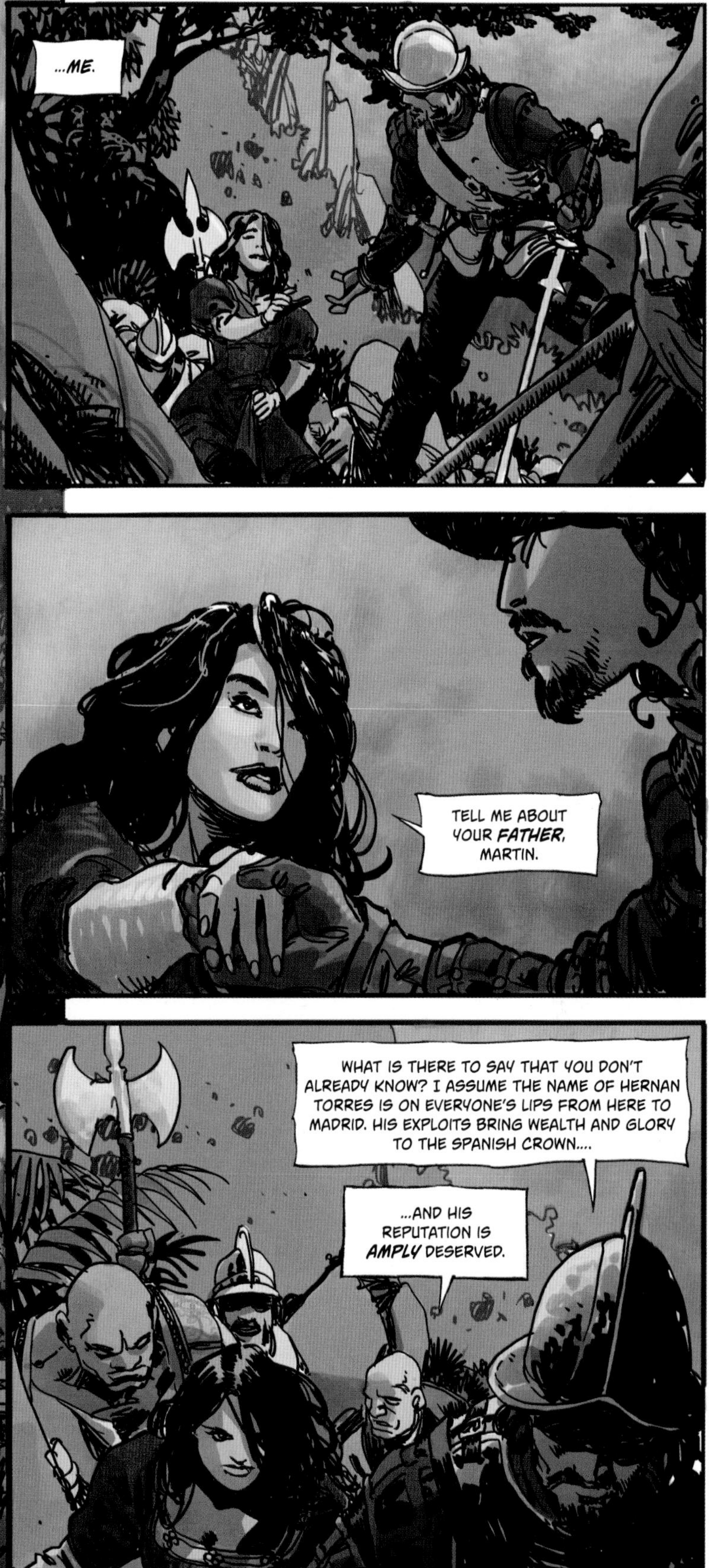
...ME.
TELL ME ABOUT YOUR FATHER, MARTIN.
WHAT IS THERE TO SAY THAT YOU DON'T ALREADY KNOW? I ASSUME THE NAME OF HERNAN TORRES IS ON EVERYONE'S LIPS FROM HERE TO MADRID. HIS EXPLOITS BRING WEALTH AND GLORY TO THE SPANISH CROWN....
...AND HIS REPUTATION IS AMPLY DESERVED.

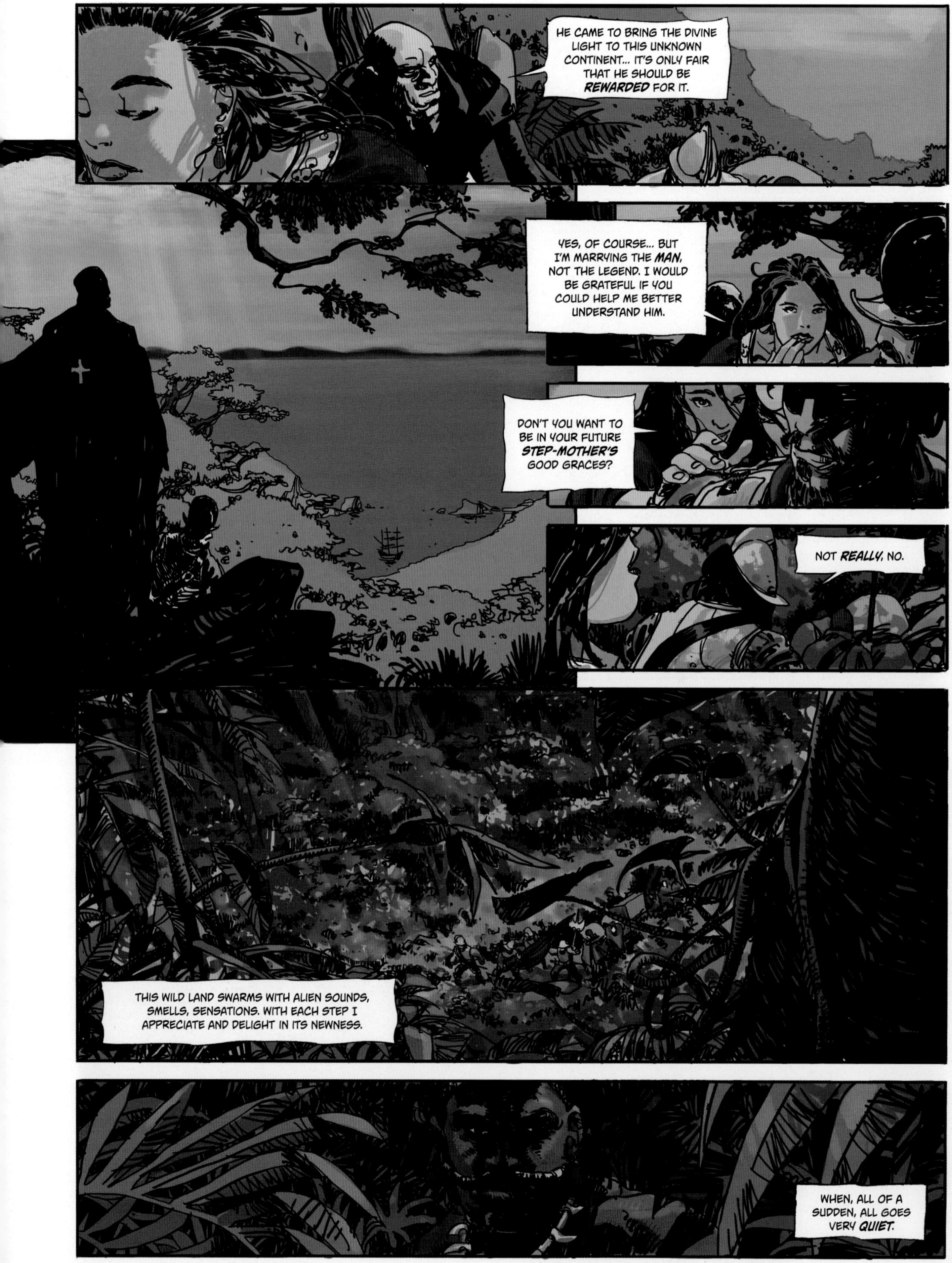
HE CAME TO BRING THE DIVINE LIGHT TO THIS UNKNOWN CONTINENT... IT'S ONLY FAIR THAT HE SHOULD BE **REWARDED** FOR IT.
YES, OF COURSE... BUT I'M MARRYING THE **MAN**, NOT THE LEGEND. I WOULD BE GRATEFUL IF YOU COULD HELP ME BETTER UNDERSTAND HIM.
DON'T YOU WANT TO BE IN YOUR FUTURE **STEP-MOTHER'S** GOOD GRACES?
NOT **REALLY**, NO.
THIS WILD LAND SWARMS WITH ALIEN SOUNDS, SMELLS, SENSATIONS. WITH EACH STEP I APPRECIATE AND DELIGHT IN ITS NEWNESS.
WHEN, ALL OF A SUDDEN, ALL GOES VERY **QUIET**.

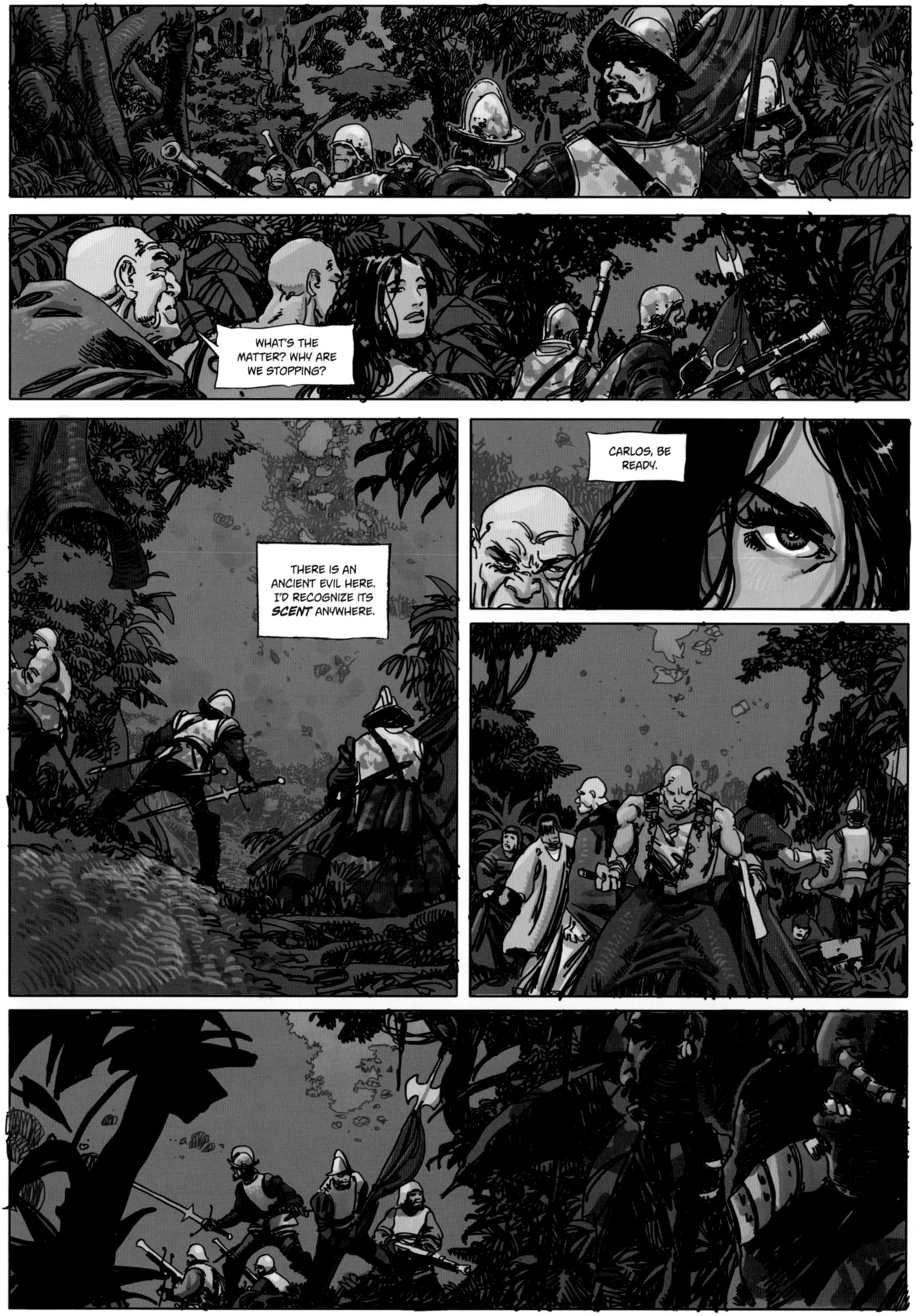
WHAT'S THE MATTER? WHY ARE WE STOPPING?
THERE IS AN ANCIENT EVIL HERE. I'D RECOGNIZE ITS SCENT ANYWHERE.
CARLOS, BE READY.

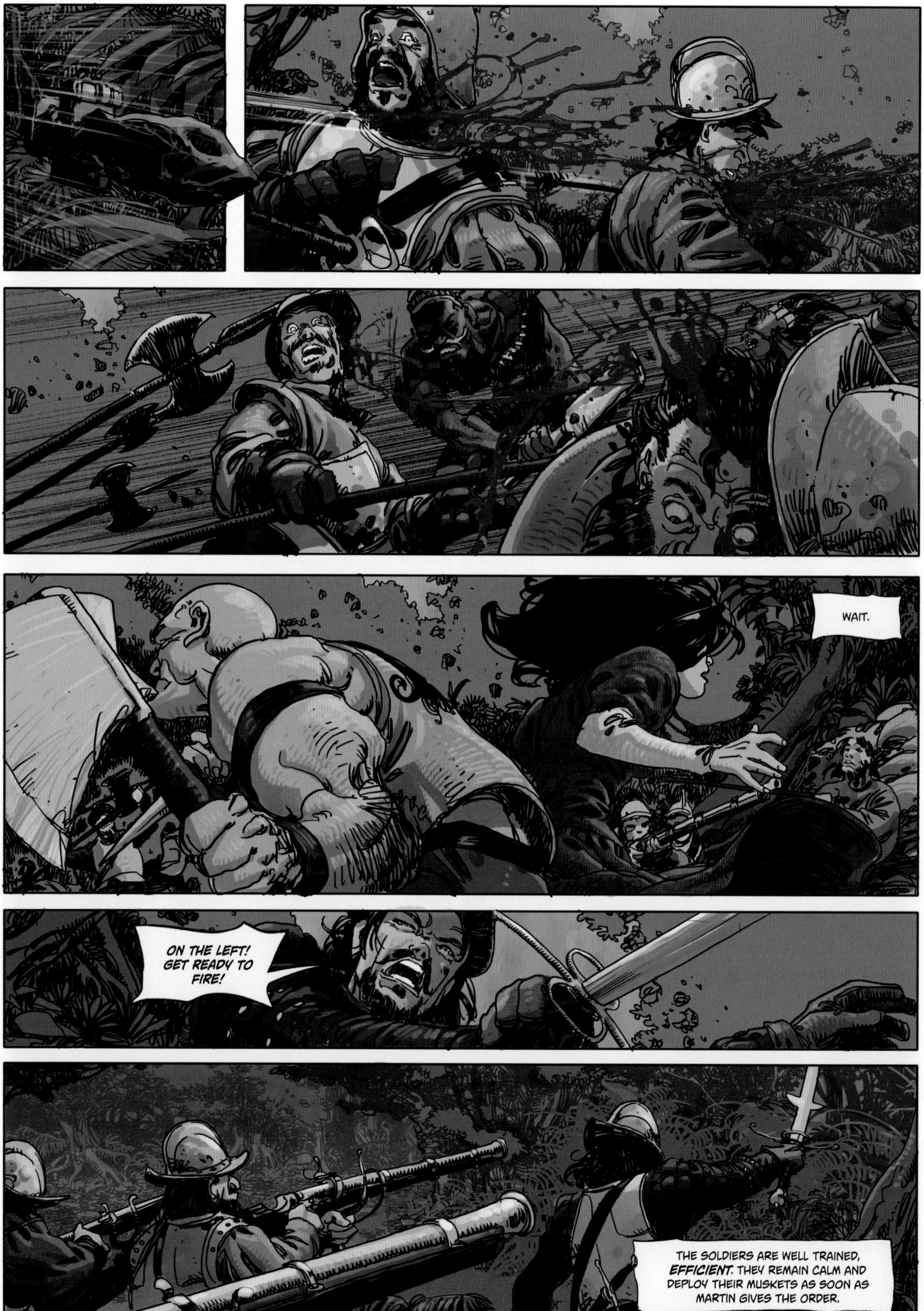
WAIT.
ON THE LEFT! GET READY TO FIRE!
THE SOLDIERS ARE WELL TRAINED, *EFFICIENT*. THEY REMAIN CALM AND DEPLOY THEIR MUSKETS AS SOON AS MARTIN GIVES THE ORDER.

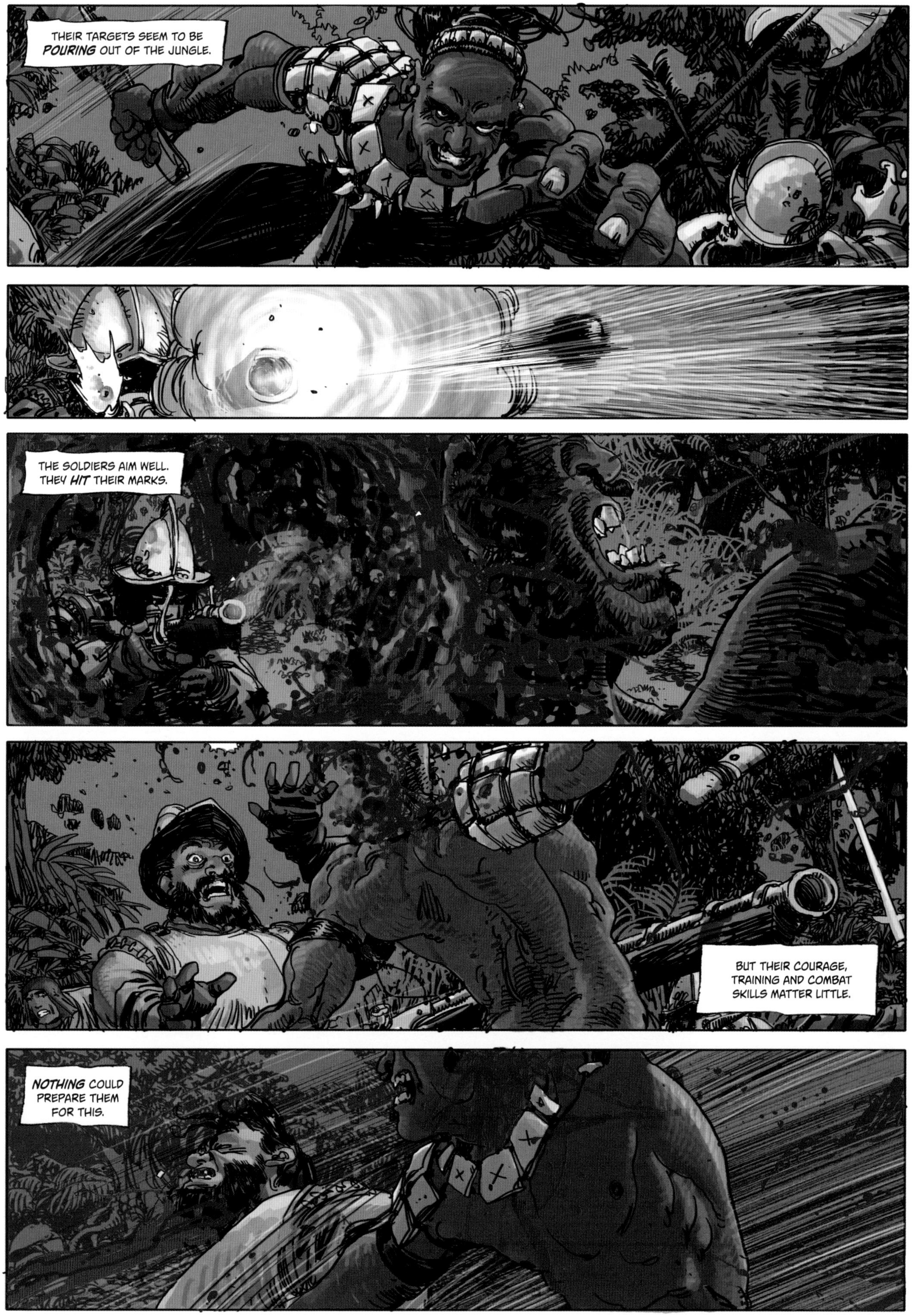
THEIR TARGETS SEEM TO BE *POURING* OUT OF THE JUNGLE.
THE SOLDIERS AIM WELL. THEY *HIT* THEIR MARKS.
BUT THEIR COURAGE, TRAINING AND COMBAT SKILLS MATTER LITTLE.
NOTHING COULD PREPARE THEM FOR THIS.

NOW.

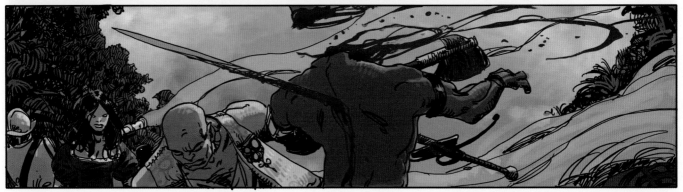

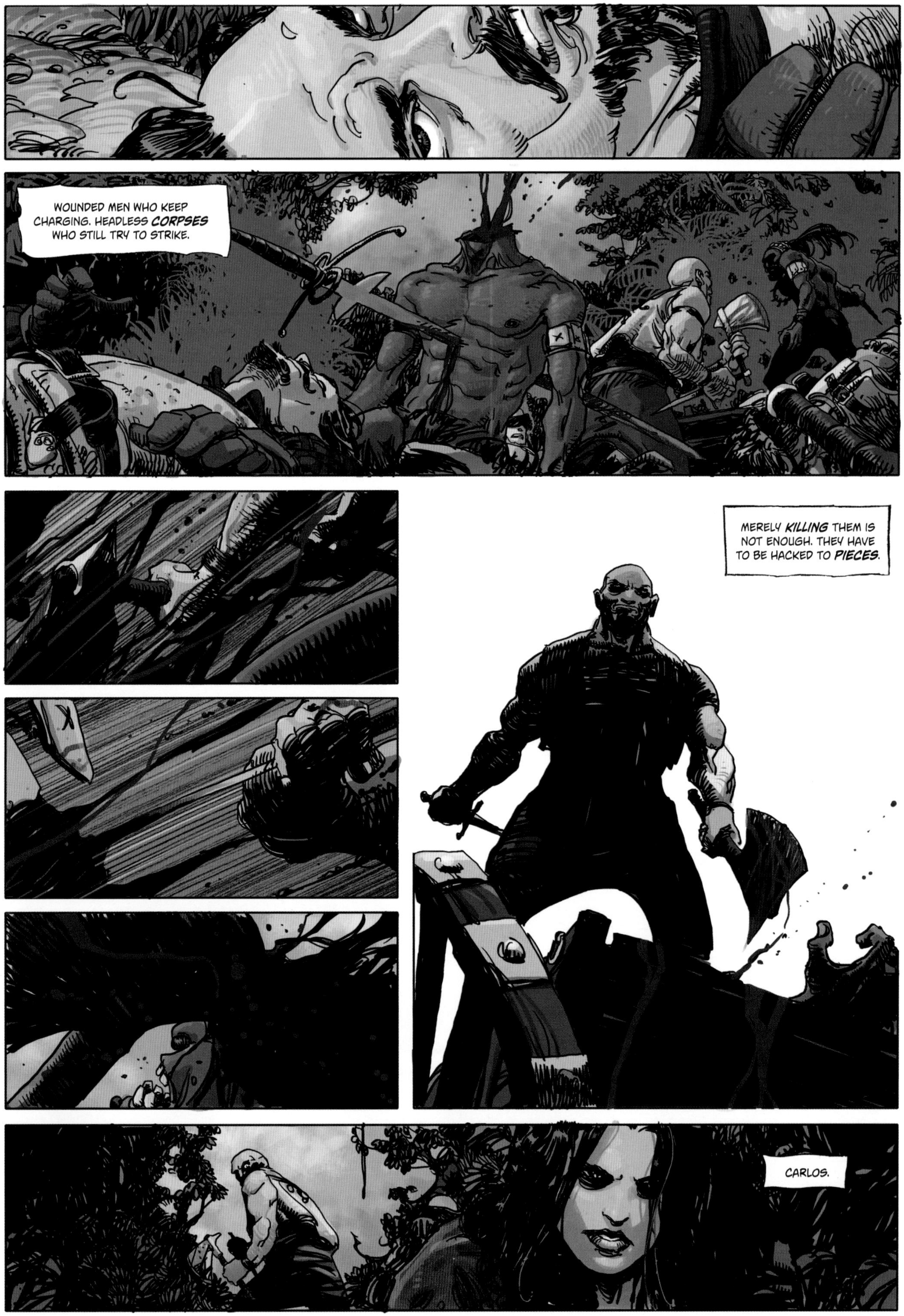
WOUNDED MEN WHO KEEP CHARGING. HEADLESS CORPSES WHO STILL TRY TO STRIKE.
MERELY KILLING THEM IS NOT ENOUGH. THEY HAVE TO BE HACKED TO PIECES.
CARLOS.

THE LAST ONE FACES ME. HE WANTS TO PLAY. HAS HE *RECOGNIZED* ME?

I DON'T EVEN NEED TO LOOK AT HIS NECK...

...TO KNOW WHAT *SIGN* IT BEARS.

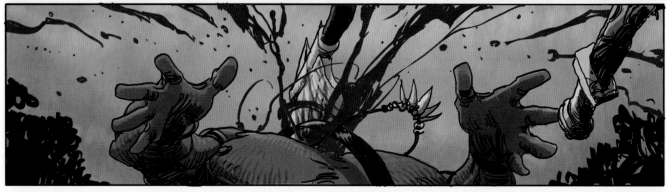

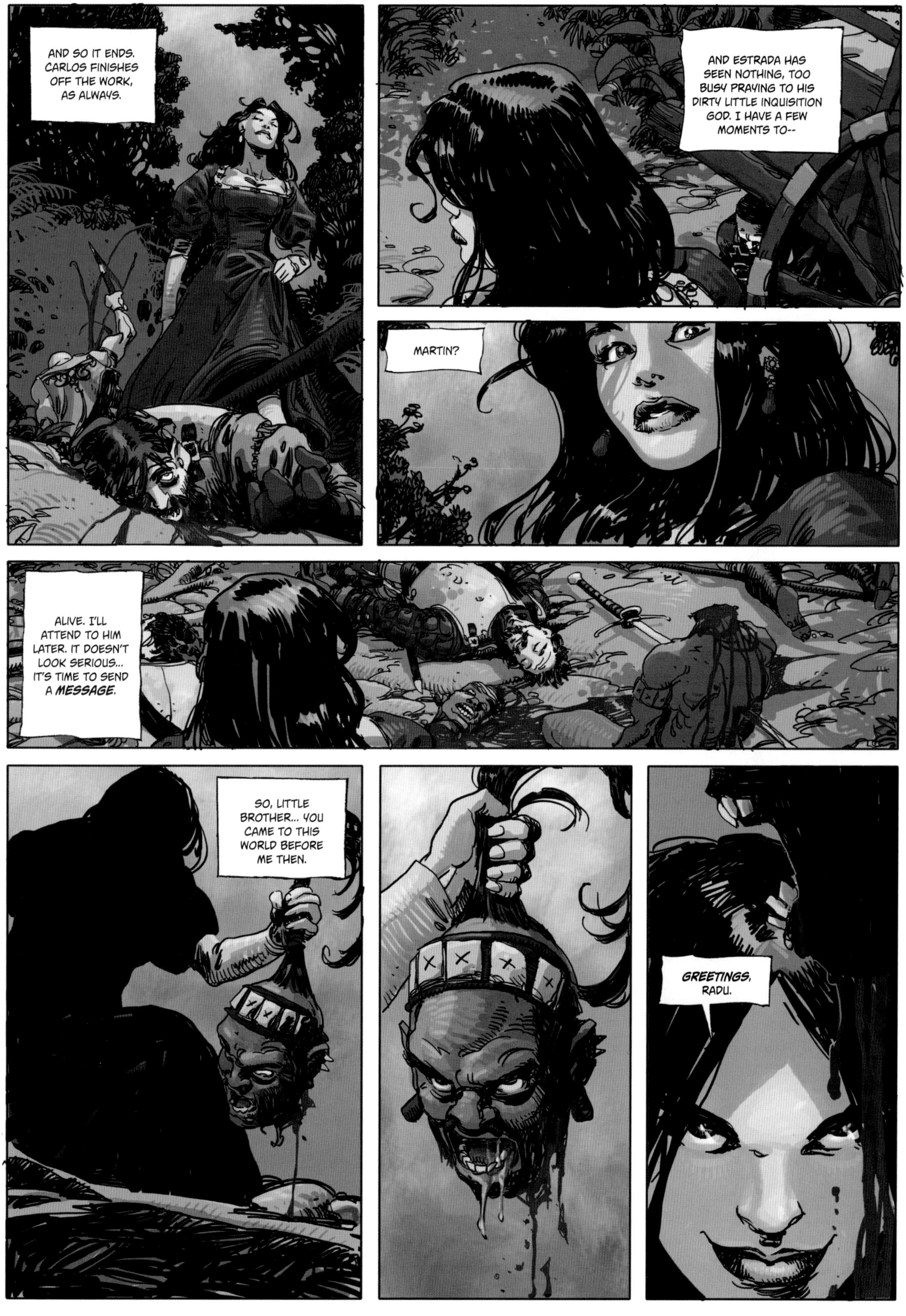
AND SO IT ENDS. CARLOS FINISHES OFF THE WORK, AS ALWAYS.
AND ESTRADA HAS SEEN NOTHING, TOO BUSY PRAYING TO HIS DIRTY LITTLE INQUISITION GOD. I HAVE A FEW MOMENTS TO--
MARTIN?
ALIVE. I'LL ATTEND TO HIM LATER. IT DOESN'T LOOK SERIOUS... IT'S TIME TO SEND A *MESSAGE*.
SO, LITTLE BROTHER... YOU CAME TO THIS WORLD BEFORE ME THEN.
GREETINGS, RADU.

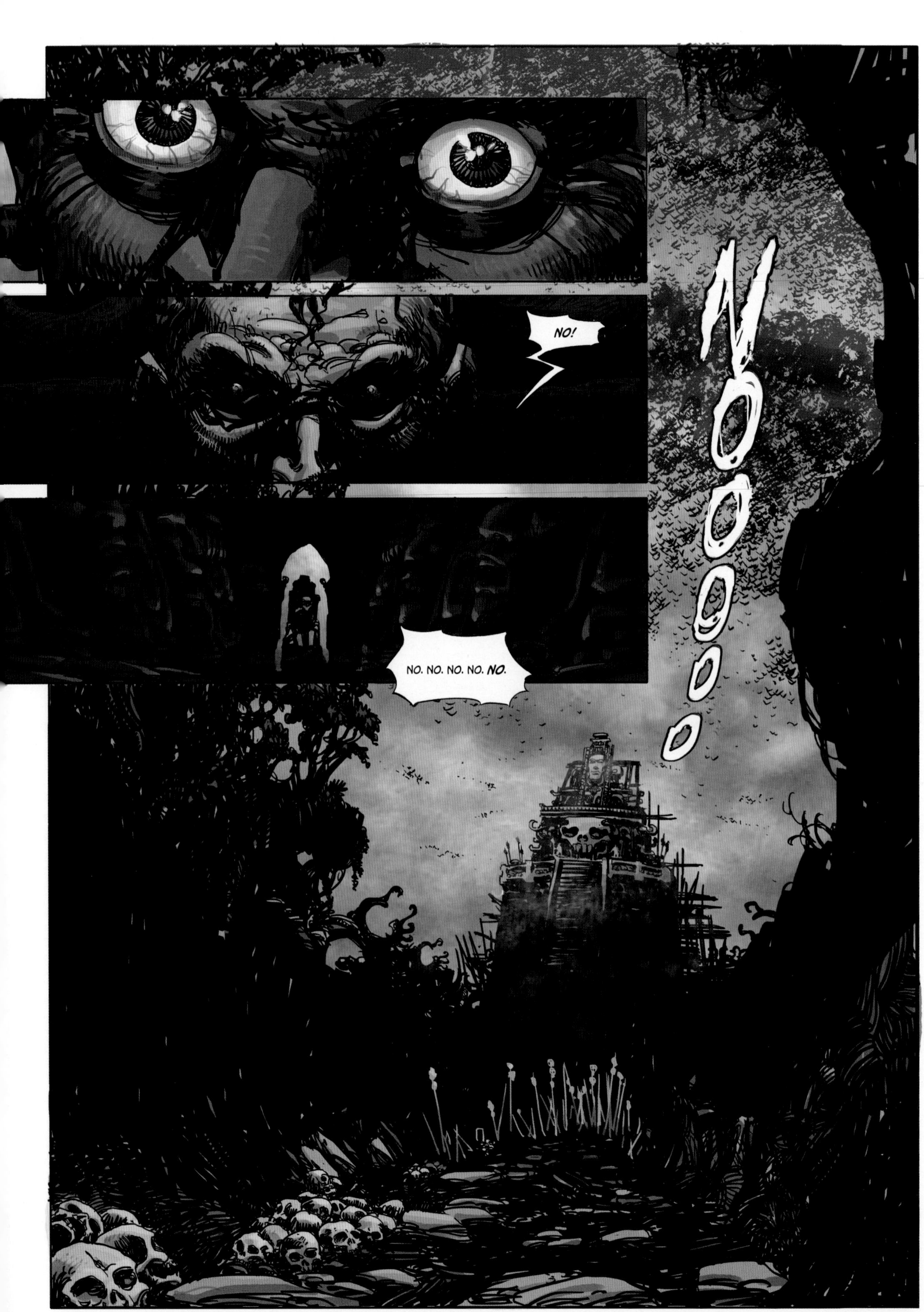
NO!
NO. NO. NO. NO. NO.
NOOOOOOO

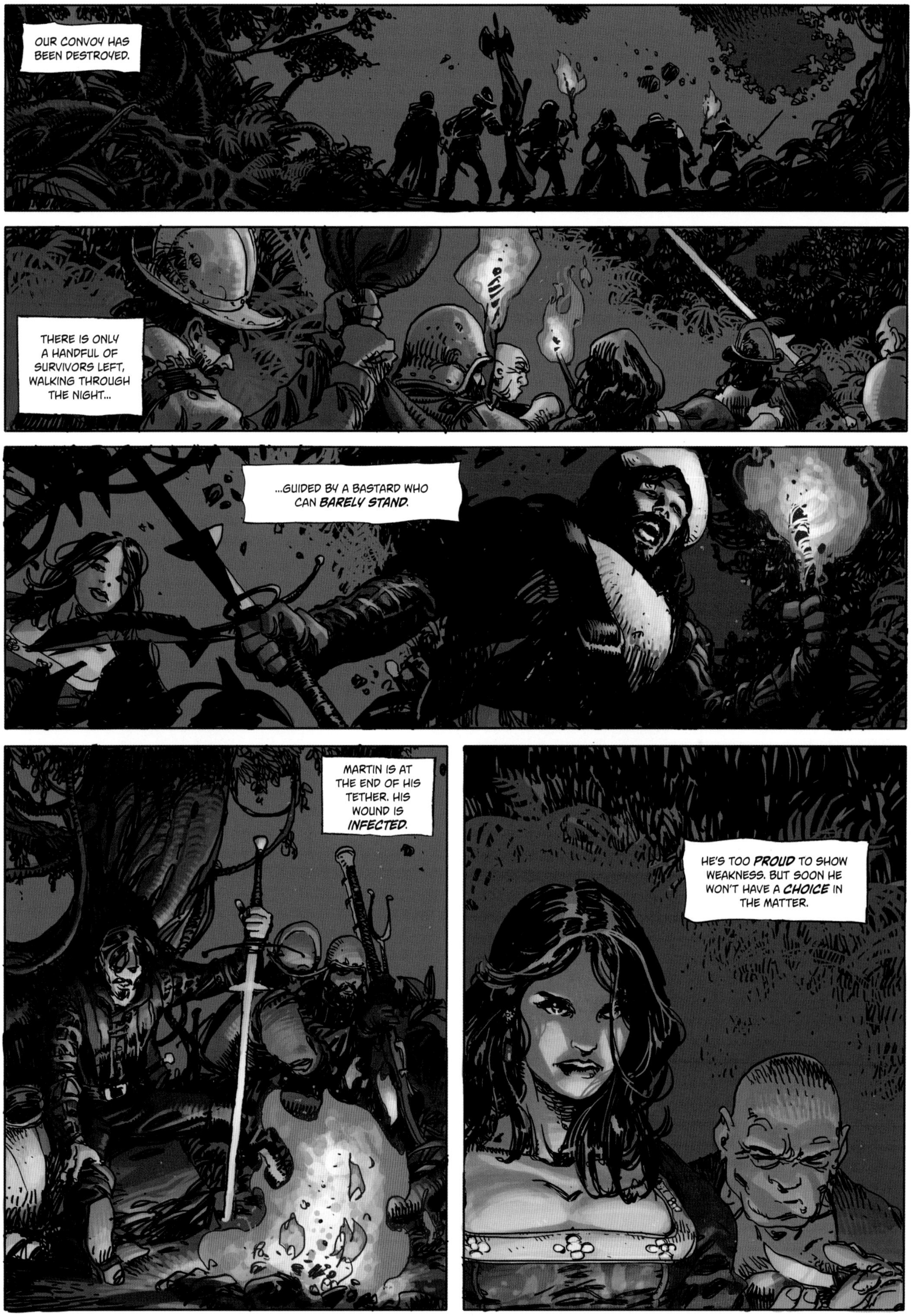
OUR CONVOY HAS BEEN DESTROYED.
THERE IS ONLY A HANDFUL OF SURVIVORS LEFT, WALKING THROUGH THE NIGHT...
...GUIDED BY A BASTARD WHO CAN BARELY STAND.
MARTIN IS AT THE END OF HIS TETHER. HIS WOUND IS INFECTED.
HE'S TOO PROUD TO SHOW WEAKNESS. BUT SOON HE WON'T HAVE A CHOICE IN THE MATTER.

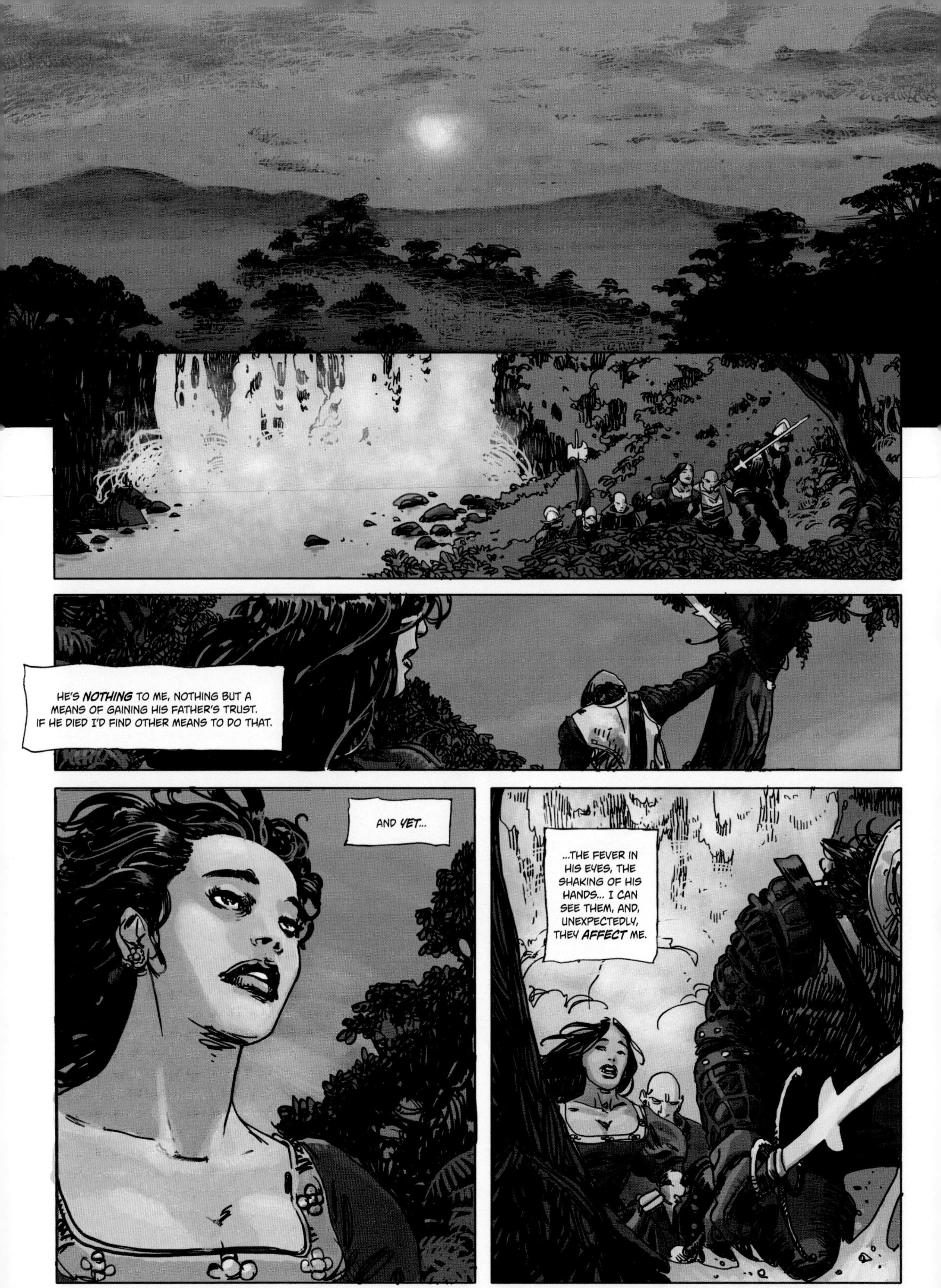
HE'S NOTHING TO ME, NOTHING BUT A MEANS OF GAINING HIS FATHER'S TRUST. IF HE DIED I'D FIND OTHER MEANS TO DO THAT.
AND YET...
...THE FEVER IN HIS EYES, THE SHAKING OF HIS HANDS... I CAN SEE THEM, AND, UNEXPECTEDLY, THEY AFFECT ME.

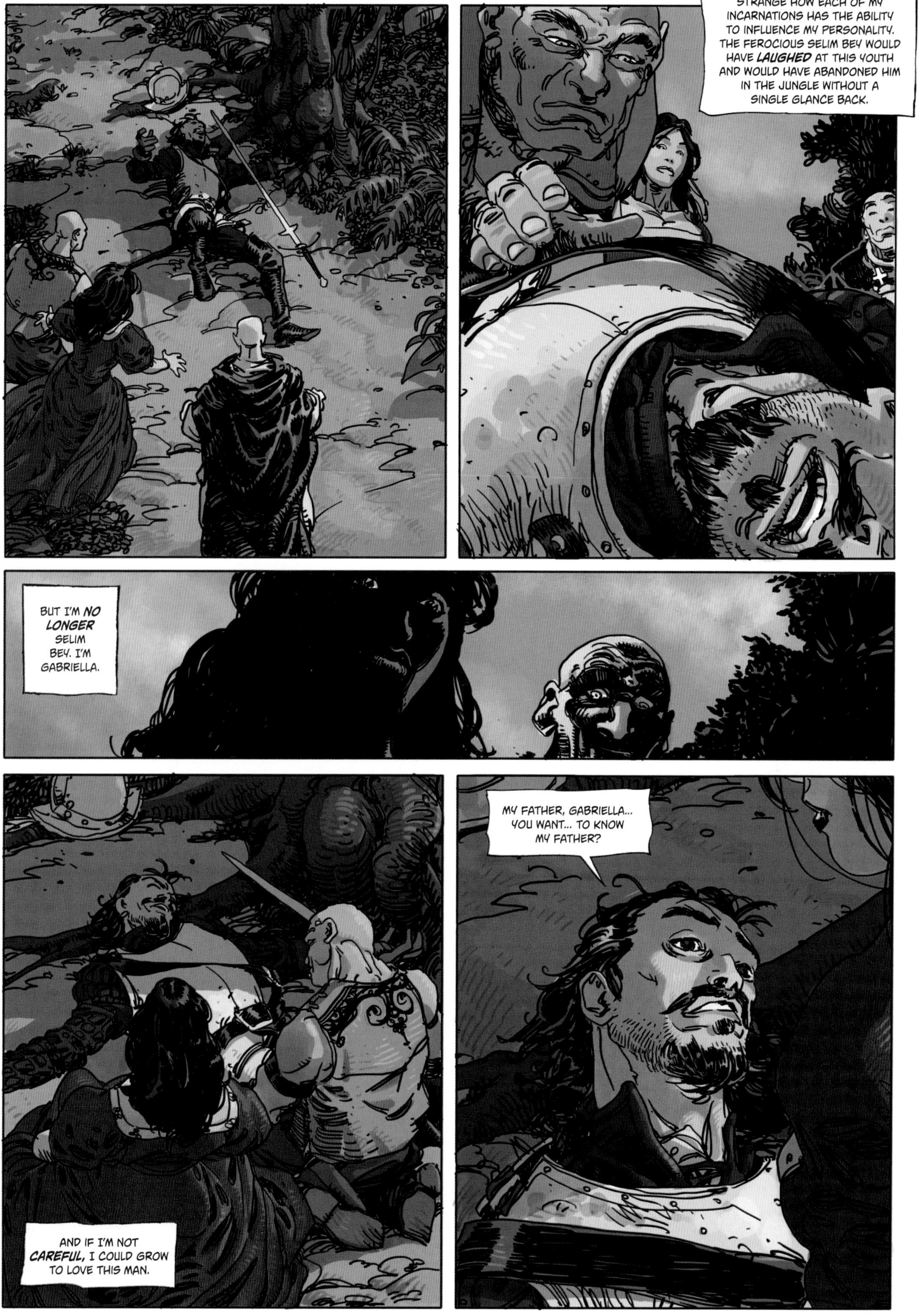
STRANGE HOW EACH OF MY INCARNATIONS HAS THE ABILITY TO INFLUENCE MY PERSONALITY. THE FEROCIOUS SELIM BEY WOULD HAVE LAUGHED AT THIS YOUTH AND WOULD HAVE ABANDONED HIM IN THE JUNGLE WITHOUT A SINGLE GLANCE BACK.
BUT I'M NO LONGER SELIM BEY. I'M GABRIELLA.
AND IF I'M NOT CAREFUL, I COULD GROW TO LOVE THIS MAN.
MY FATHER, GABRIELLA... YOU WANT... TO KNOW MY FATHER?

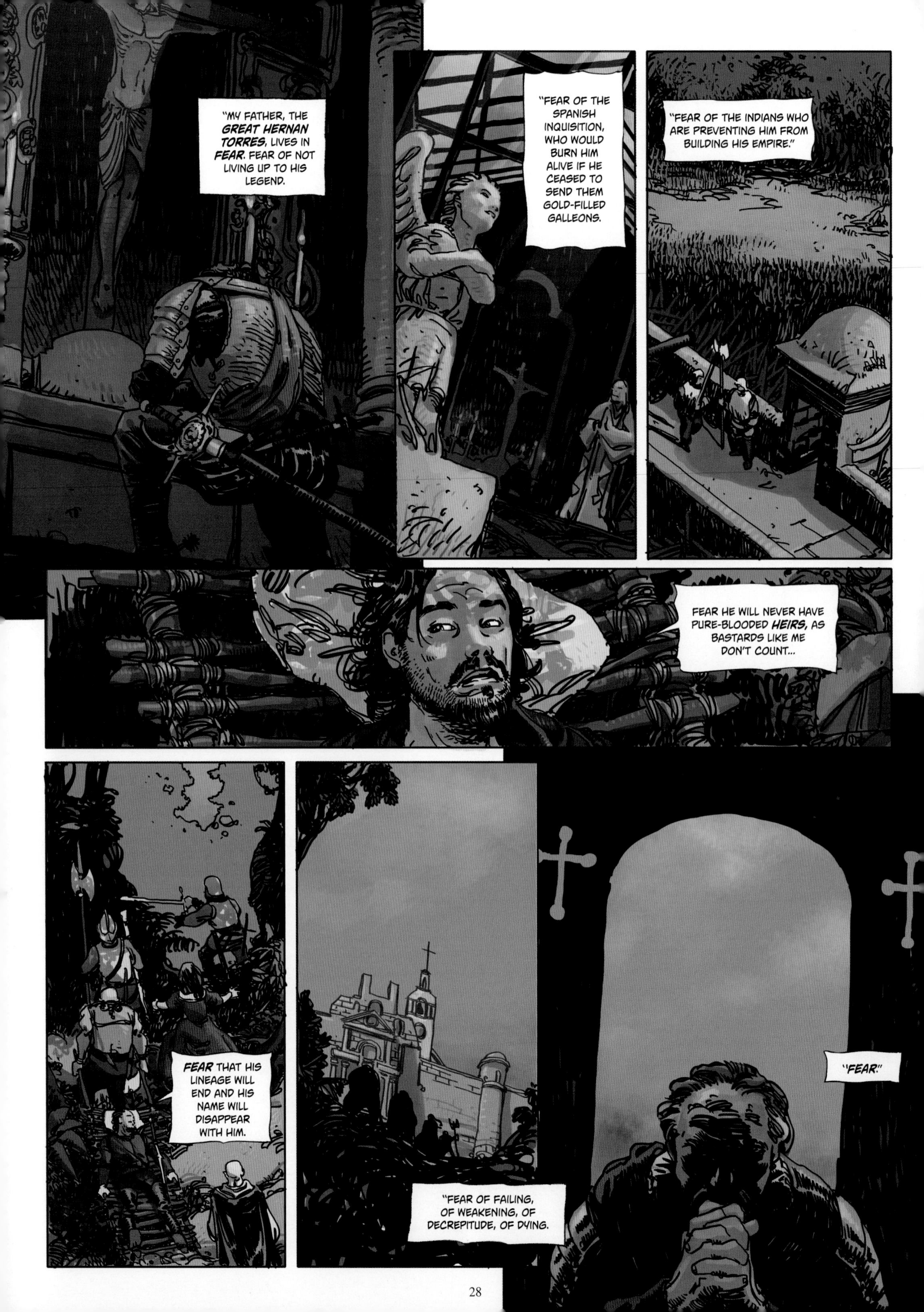
"MY FATHER, THE **GREAT HERNAN TORRES**, LIVES IN **FEAR**. FEAR OF NOT LIVING UP TO HIS LEGEND.
"FEAR OF THE SPANISH INQUISITION, WHO WOULD BURN HIM ALIVE IF HE CEASED TO SEND THEM GOLD-FILLED GALLEONS.
"FEAR OF THE INDIANS WHO ARE PREVENTING HIM FROM BUILDING HIS EMPIRE."
FEAR HE WILL NEVER HAVE PURE-BLOODED **HEIRS**, AS BASTARDS LIKE ME DON'T COUNT...
FEAR THAT HIS LINEAGE WILL END AND HIS NAME WILL DISAPPEAR WITH HIM.
"FEAR OF FAILING, OF WEAKENING, OF DECREPITUDE, OF DYING.
"**FEAR**."

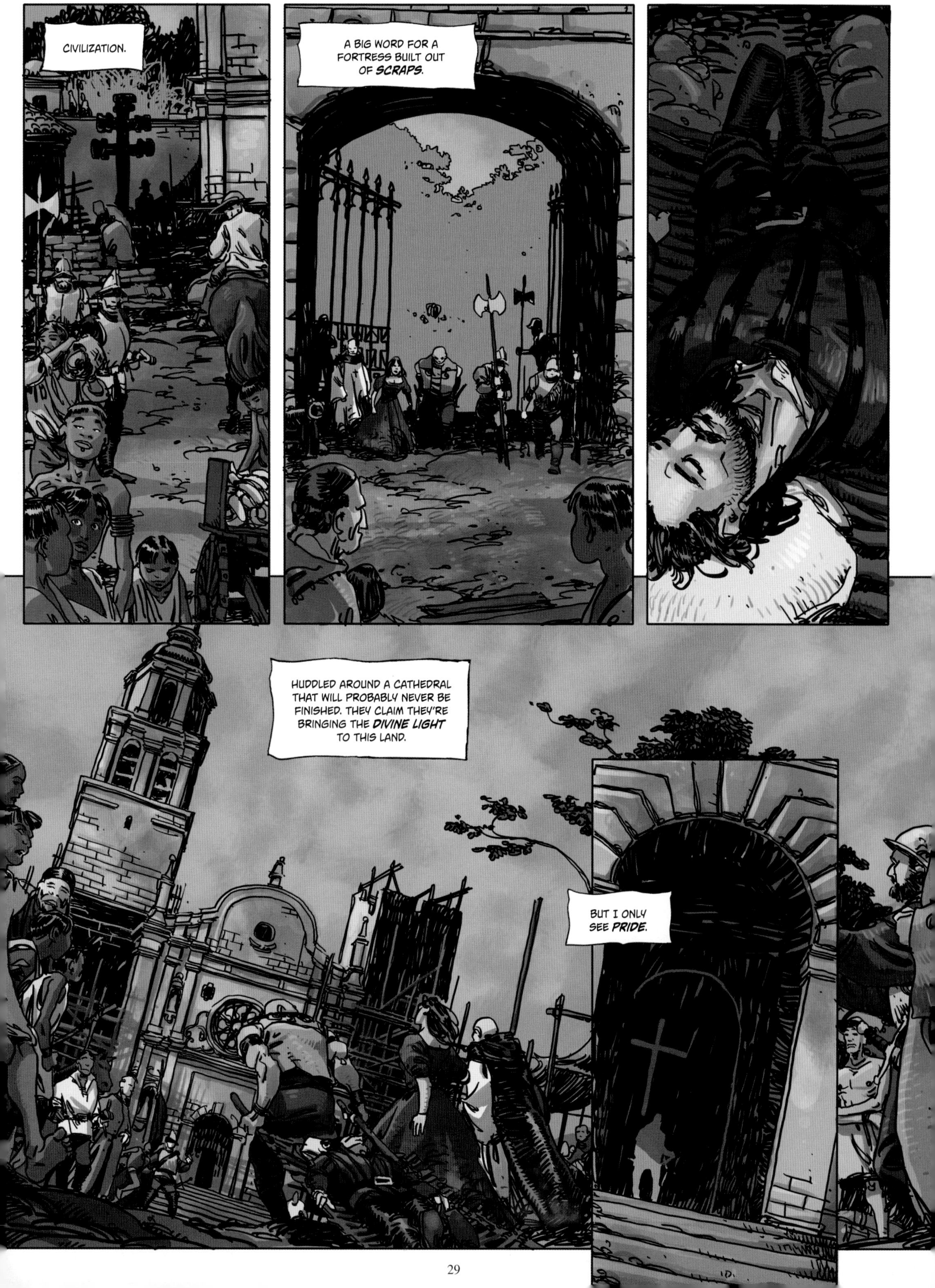
CIVILIZATION.
A BIG WORD FOR A FORTRESS BUILT OUT OF SCRAPS.
HUDDLED AROUND A CATHEDRAL THAT WILL PROBABLY NEVER BE FINISHED. THEY CLAIM THEY'RE BRINGING THE DIVINE LIGHT TO THIS LAND.
BUT I ONLY SEE PRIDE.

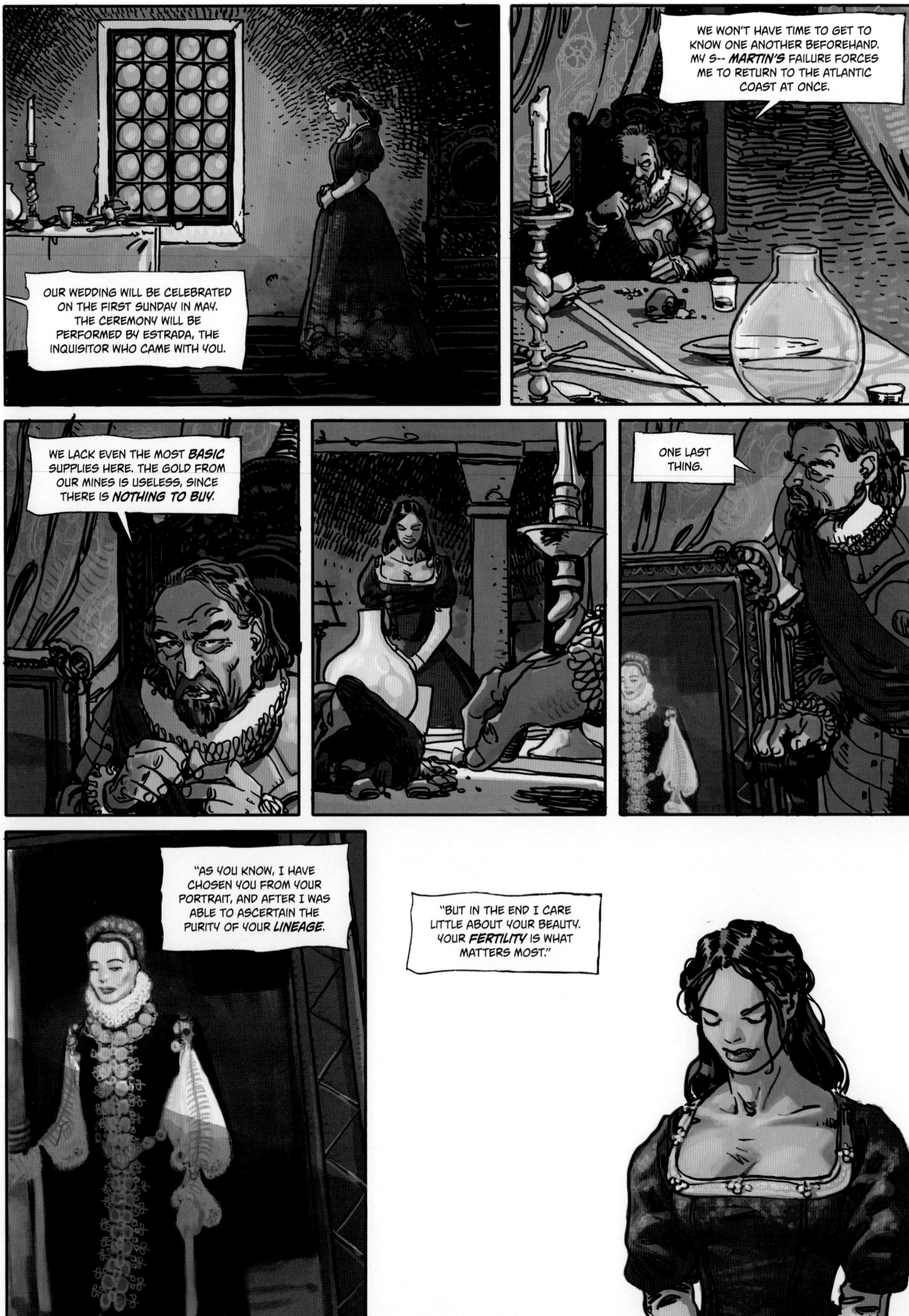
OUR WEDDING WILL BE CELEBRATED ON THE FIRST SUNDAY IN MAY. THE CEREMONY WILL BE PERFORMED BY ESTRADA, THE INQUISITOR WHO CAME WITH YOU.
WE WON'T HAVE TIME TO GET TO KNOW ONE ANOTHER BEFOREHAND. MY S-- MARTIN'S FAILURE FORCES ME TO RETURN TO THE ATLANTIC COAST AT ONCE.
WE LACK EVEN THE MOST BASIC SUPPLIES HERE. THE GOLD FROM OUR MINES IS USELESS, SINCE THERE IS NOTHING TO BUY.
ONE LAST THING.
"AS YOU KNOW, I HAVE CHOSEN YOU FROM YOUR PORTRAIT, AND AFTER I WAS ABLE TO ASCERTAIN THE PURITY OF YOUR LINEAGE.
"BUT IN THE END I CARE LITTLE ABOUT YOUR BEAUTY. YOUR FERTILITY IS WHAT MATTERS MOST."

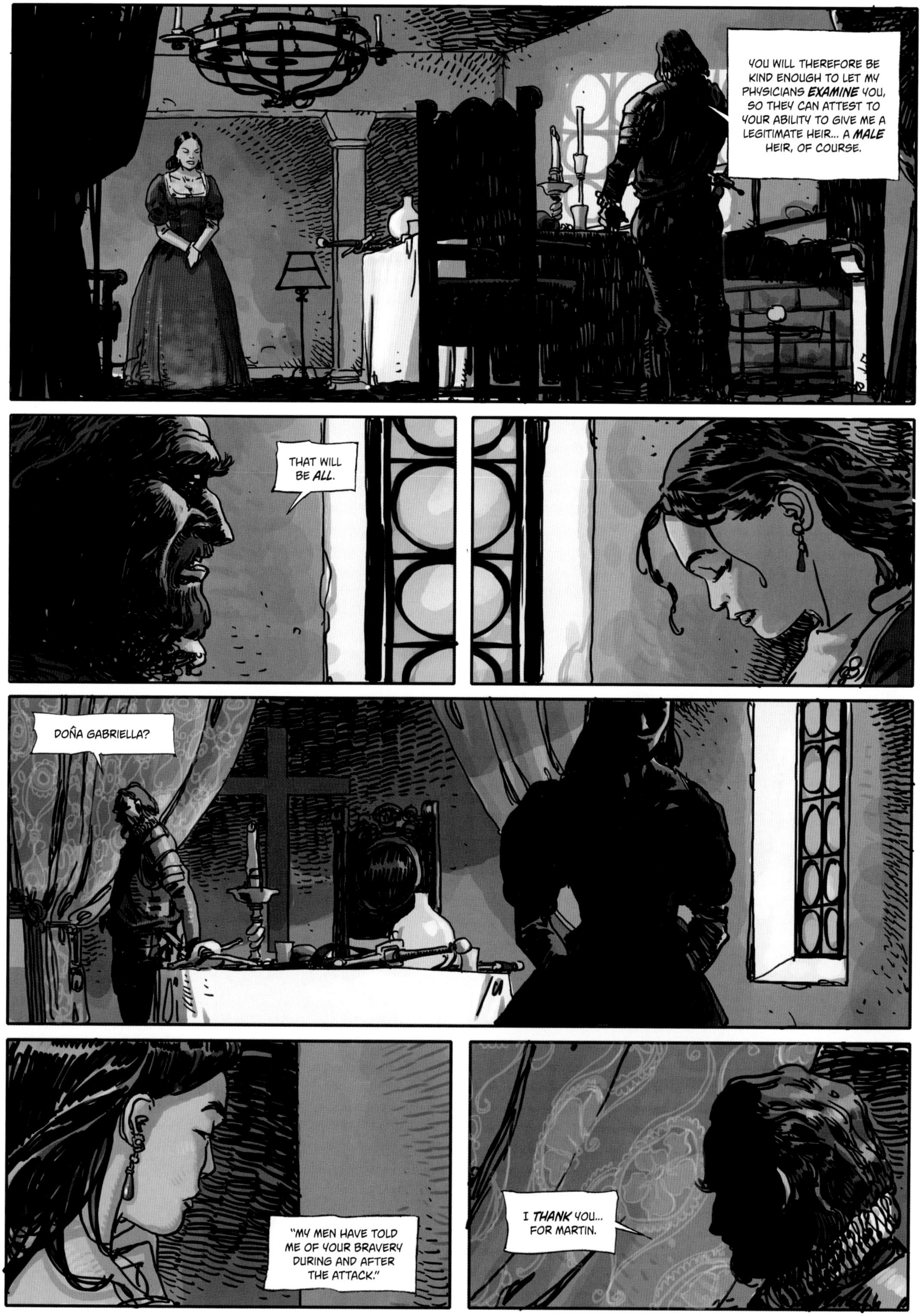
YOU WILL THEREFORE BE KIND ENOUGH TO LET MY PHYSICIANS EXAMINE YOU, SO THEY CAN ATTEST TO YOUR ABILITY TO GIVE ME A LEGITIMATE HEIR... A MALE HEIR, OF COURSE.
THAT WILL BE ALL.
DOÑA GABRIELLA?
"MY MEN HAVE TOLD ME OF YOUR BRAVERY DURING AND AFTER THE ATTACK."
I THANK YOU... FOR MARTIN.

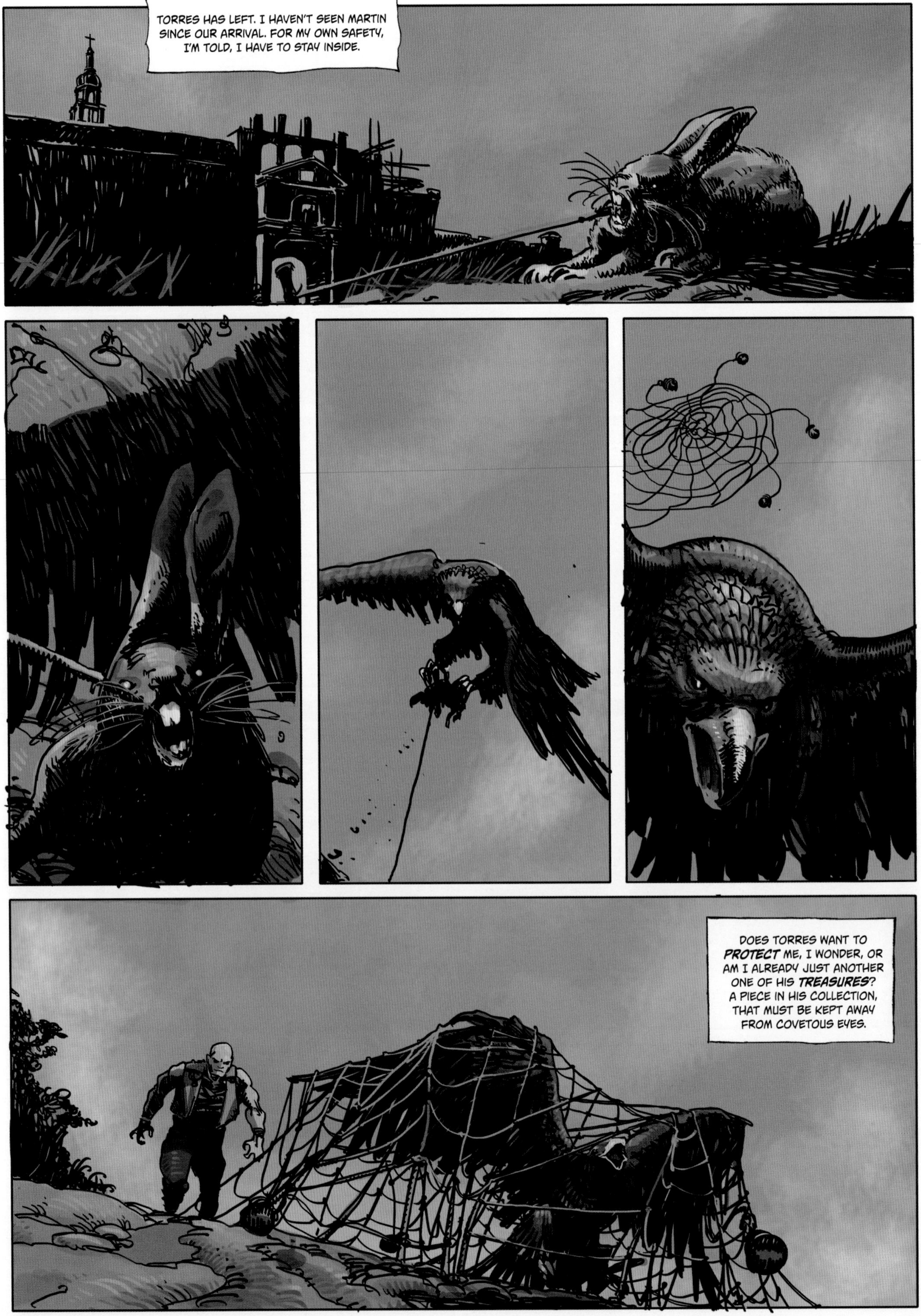
TORRES HAS LEFT. I HAVEN'T SEEN MARTIN SINCE OUR ARRIVAL. FOR MY OWN SAFETY, I'M TOLD, I HAVE TO STAY INSIDE.
DOES TORRES WANT TO *PROTECT* ME, I WONDER, OR AM I ALREADY JUST ANOTHER ONE OF HIS *TREASURES*? A PIECE IN HIS COLLECTION, THAT MUST BE KEPT AWAY FROM COVETOUS EYES.

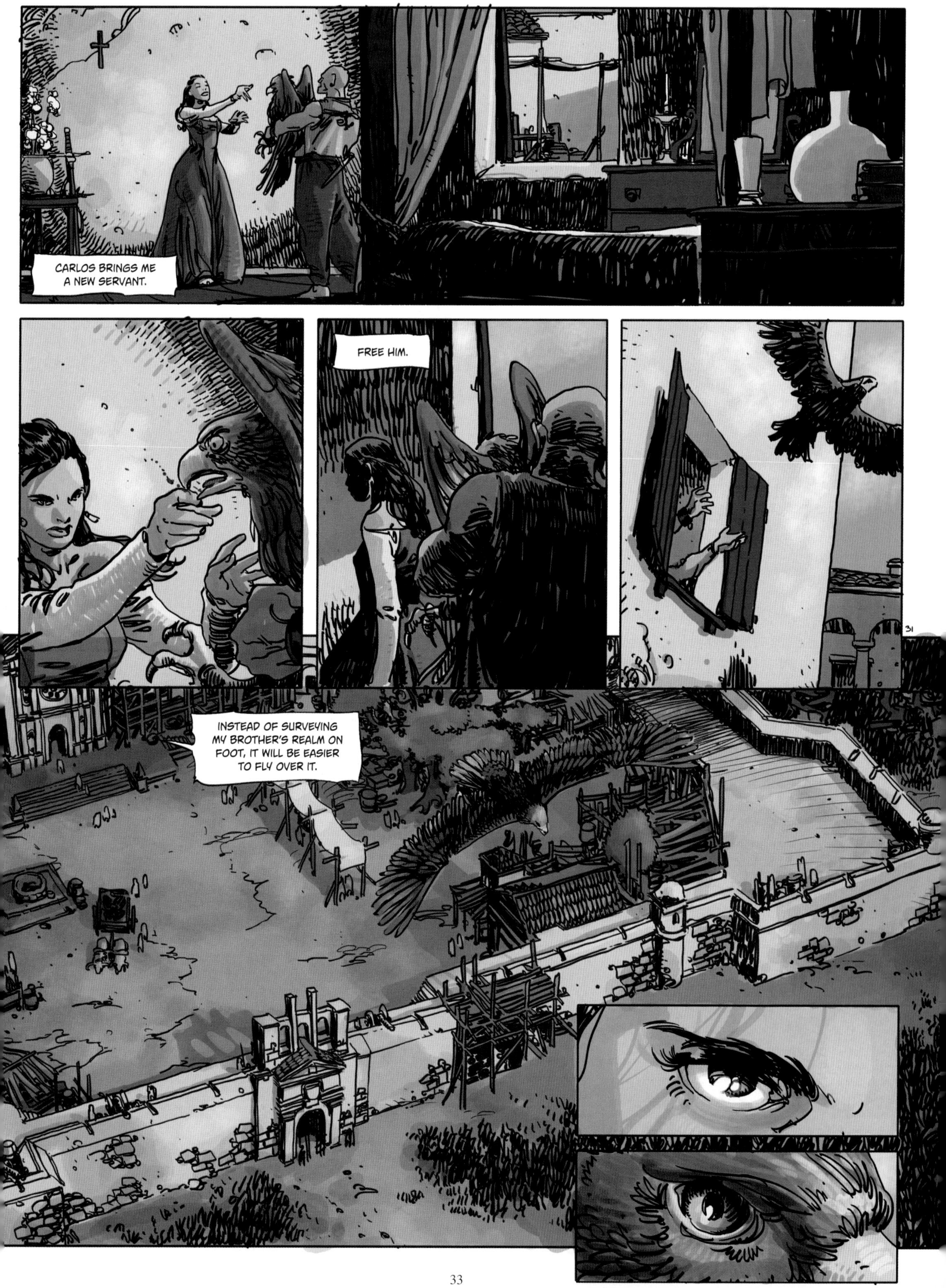
CARLOS BRINGS ME A NEW SERVANT.
FREE HIM.
31
INSTEAD OF SURVEYING MY BROTHER'S REALM ON FOOT, IT WILL BE EASIER TO FLY OVER IT.

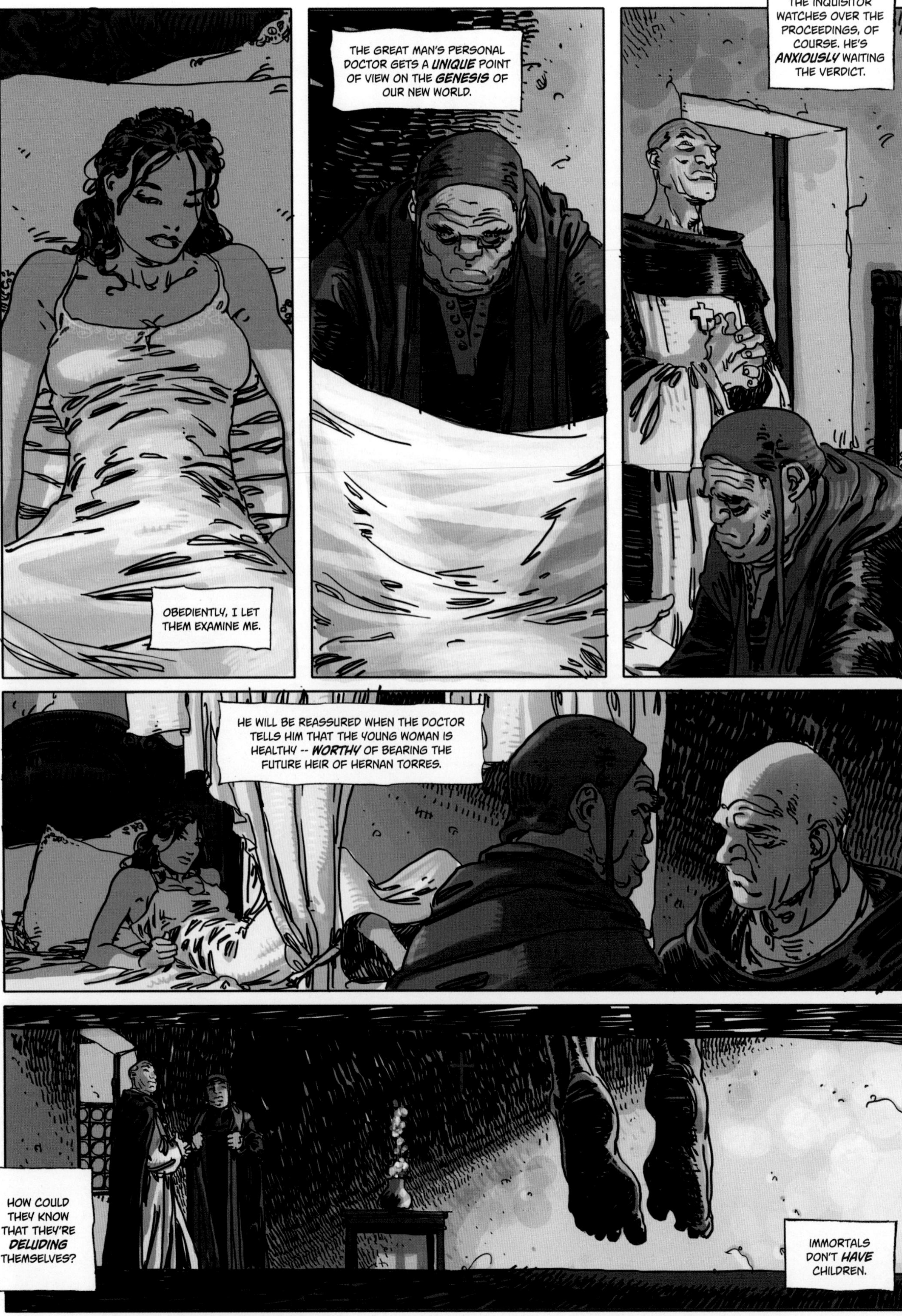
OBEDIENTLY, I LET THEM EXAMINE ME.
THE GREAT MAN'S PERSONAL DOCTOR GETS A UNIQUE POINT OF VIEW ON THE GENESIS OF OUR NEW WORLD.
THE INQUISITOR WATCHES OVER THE PROCEEDINGS, OF COURSE. HE'S ANXIOUSLY WAITING THE VERDICT.
HE WILL BE REASSURED WHEN THE DOCTOR TELLS HIM THAT THE YOUNG WOMAN IS HEALTHY -- WORTHY OF BEARING THE FUTURE HEIR OF HERNAN TORRES.
HOW COULD THEY KNOW THAT THEY'RE DELUDING THEMSELVES?
IMMORTALS DON'T HAVE CHILDREN.

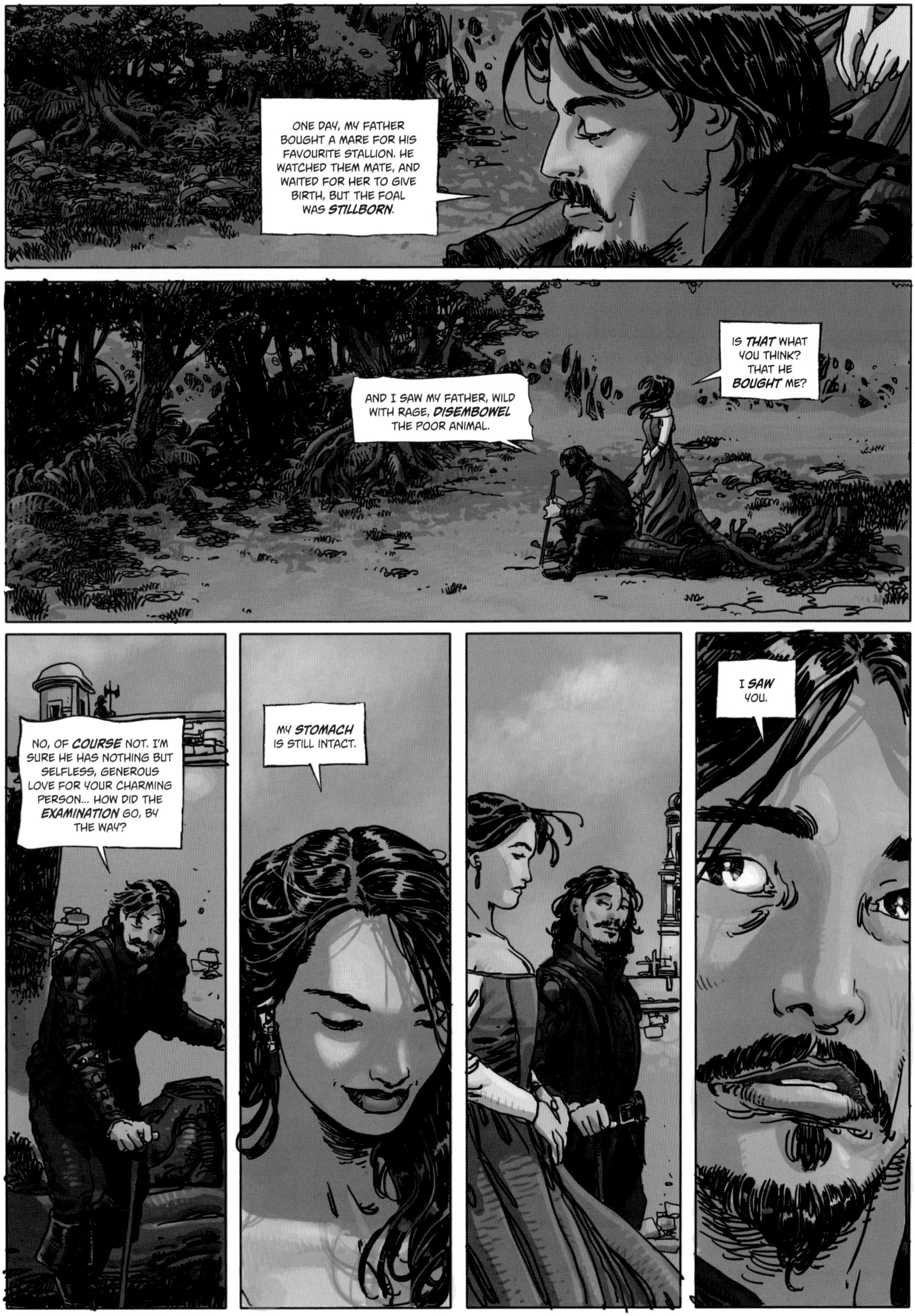
ONE DAY, MY FATHER BOUGHT A MARE FOR HIS FAVOURITE STALLION. HE WATCHED THEM MATE, AND WAITED FOR HER TO GIVE BIRTH, BUT THE FOAL WAS STILLBORN.
AND I SAW MY FATHER, WILD WITH RAGE, DISEMBOWEL THE POOR ANIMAL.
IS THAT WHAT YOU THINK? THAT HE BOUGHT ME?
NO, OF COURSE NOT. I'M SURE HE HAS NOTHING BUT SELFLESS, GENEROUS LOVE FOR YOUR CHARMING PERSON... HOW DID THE EXAMINATION GO, BY THE WAY?
MY STOMACH IS STILL INTACT.
I SAW YOU.

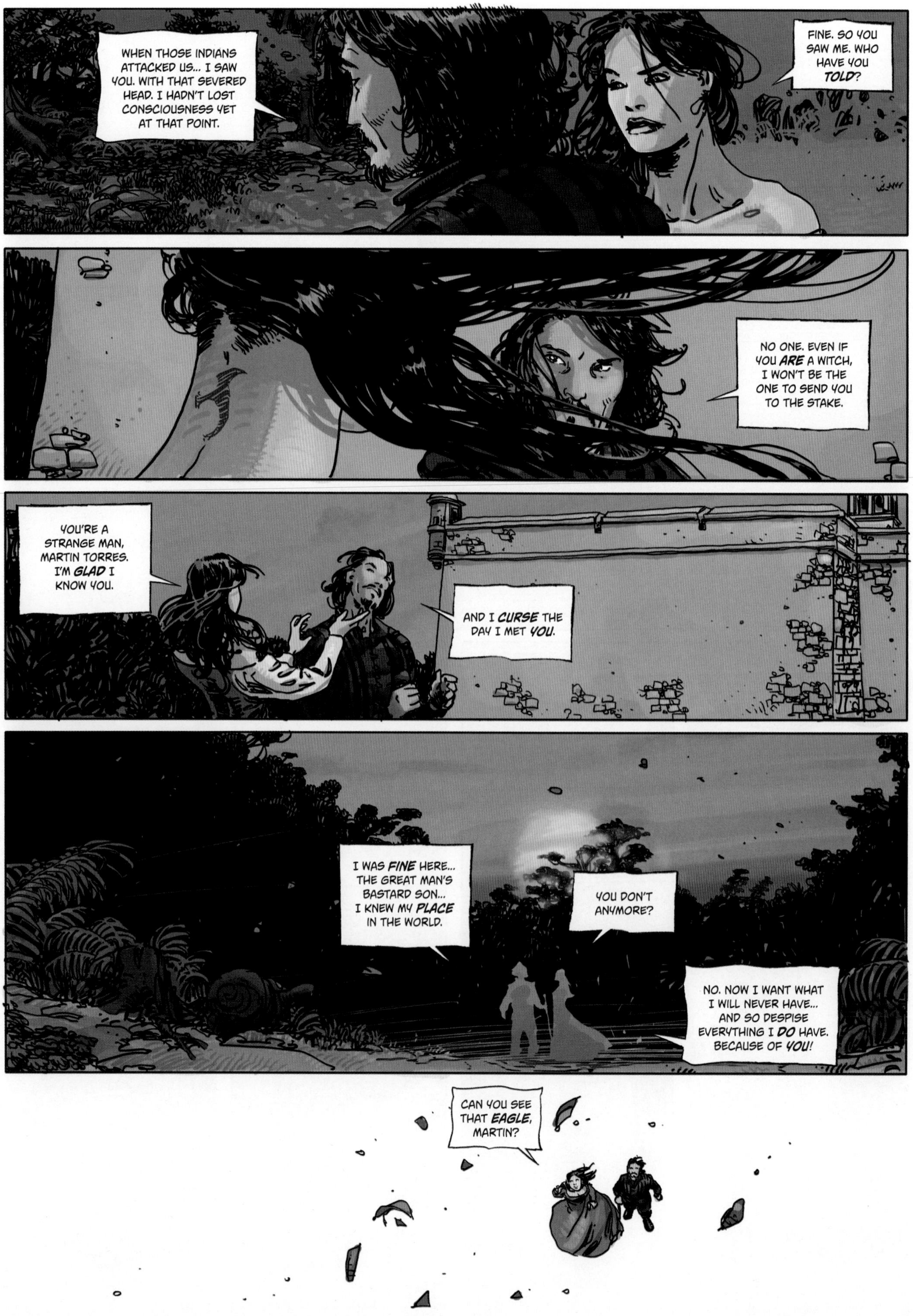
WHEN THOSE INDIANS ATTACKED US... I SAW YOU. WITH THAT SEVERED HEAD. I HADN'T LOST CONSCIOUSNESS YET AT THAT POINT.
FINE. SO YOU SAW ME. WHO HAVE YOU *TOLD*?
NO ONE. EVEN IF YOU *ARE* A WITCH, I WON'T BE THE ONE TO SEND YOU TO THE STAKE.
YOU'RE A STRANGE MAN, MARTIN TORRES. I'M *GLAD* I KNOW YOU.
AND I *CURSE* THE DAY I MET *YOU*.
I WAS *FINE* HERE... THE GREAT MAN'S BASTARD SON... I KNEW MY *PLACE* IN THE WORLD.
YOU DON'T ANYMORE?
NO. NOW I WANT WHAT I WILL NEVER HAVE... AND SO DESPISE EVERYTHING I *DO* HAVE. BECAUSE OF *YOU*!
CAN YOU SEE THAT *EAGLE*, MARTIN?

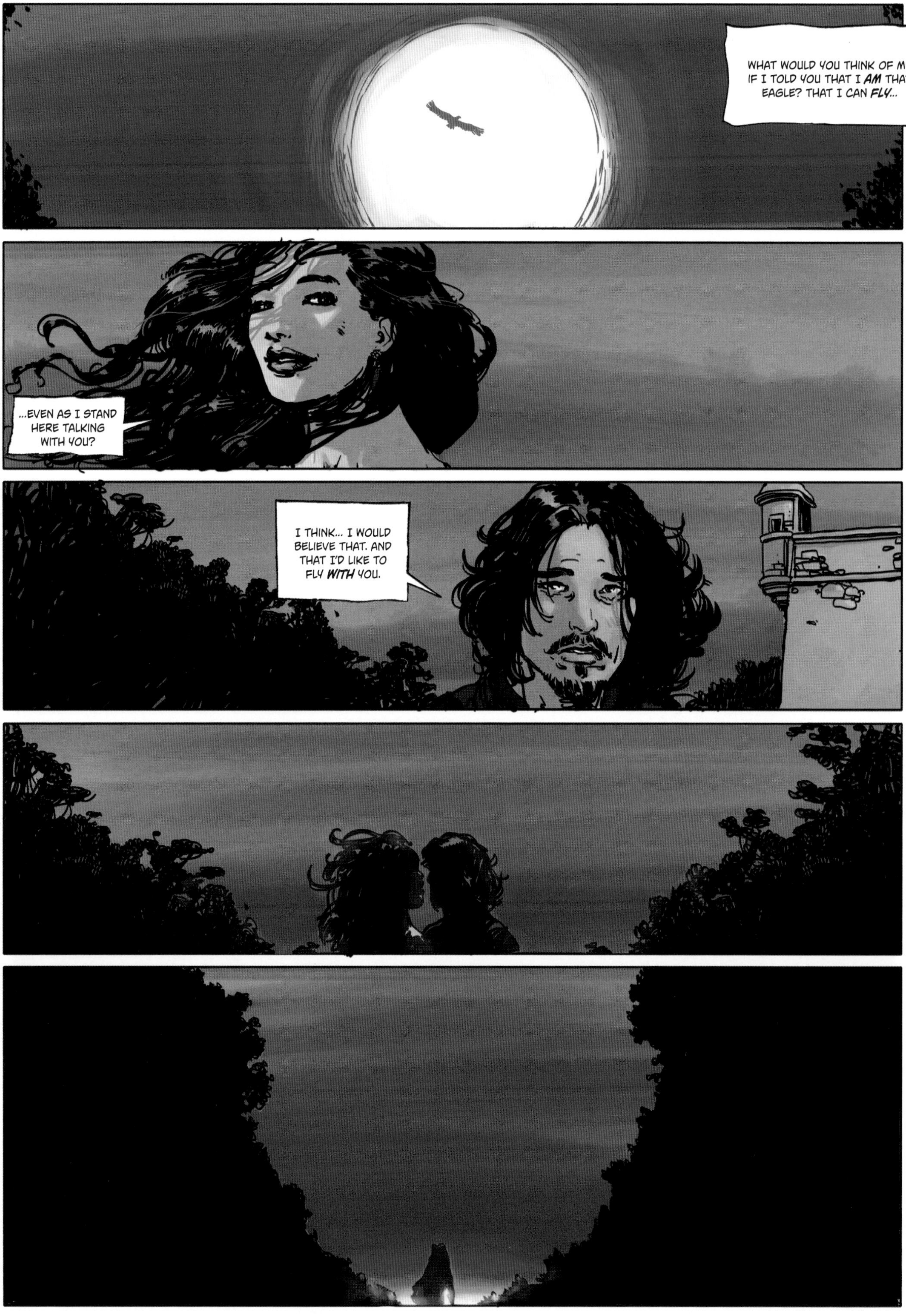
WHAT WOULD YOU THINK OF ME IF I TOLD YOU THAT I AM THAT EAGLE? THAT I CAN FLY...
...EVEN AS I STAND HERE TALKING WITH YOU?
I THINK... I WOULD BELIEVE THAT. AND THAT I'D LIKE TO FLY WITH YOU.

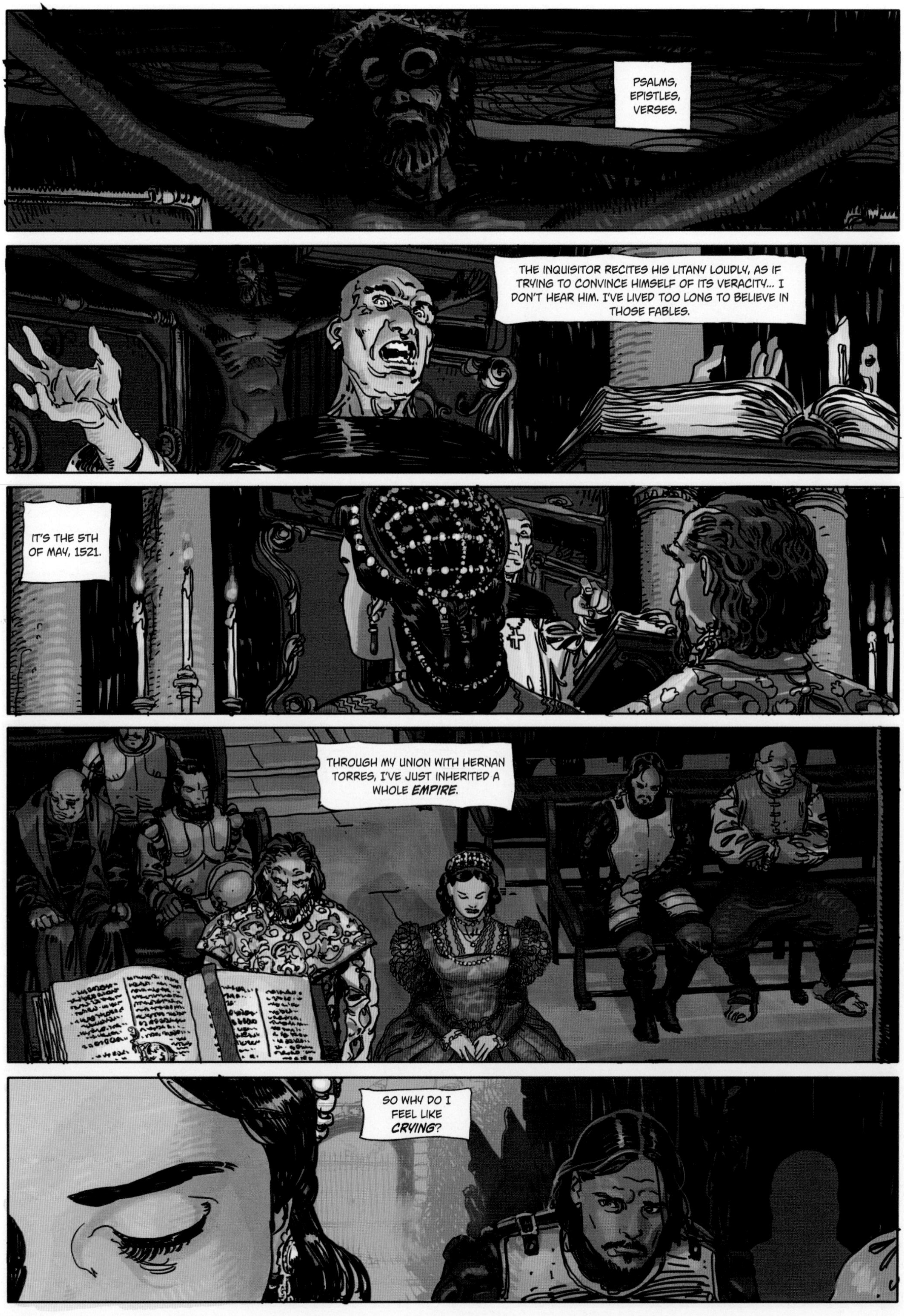
PSALMS, EPISTLES, VERSES.
THE INQUISITOR RECITES HIS LITANY LOUDLY, AS IF TRYING TO CONVINCE HIMSELF OF ITS VERACITY... I DON'T HEAR HIM. I'VE LIVED TOO LONG TO BELIEVE IN THOSE FABLES.
IT'S THE 5TH OF MAY, 1521.
THROUGH MY UNION WITH HERNAN TORRES, I'VE JUST INHERITED A WHOLE ***EMPIRE***.
SO WHY DO I FEEL LIKE ***CRYING***?

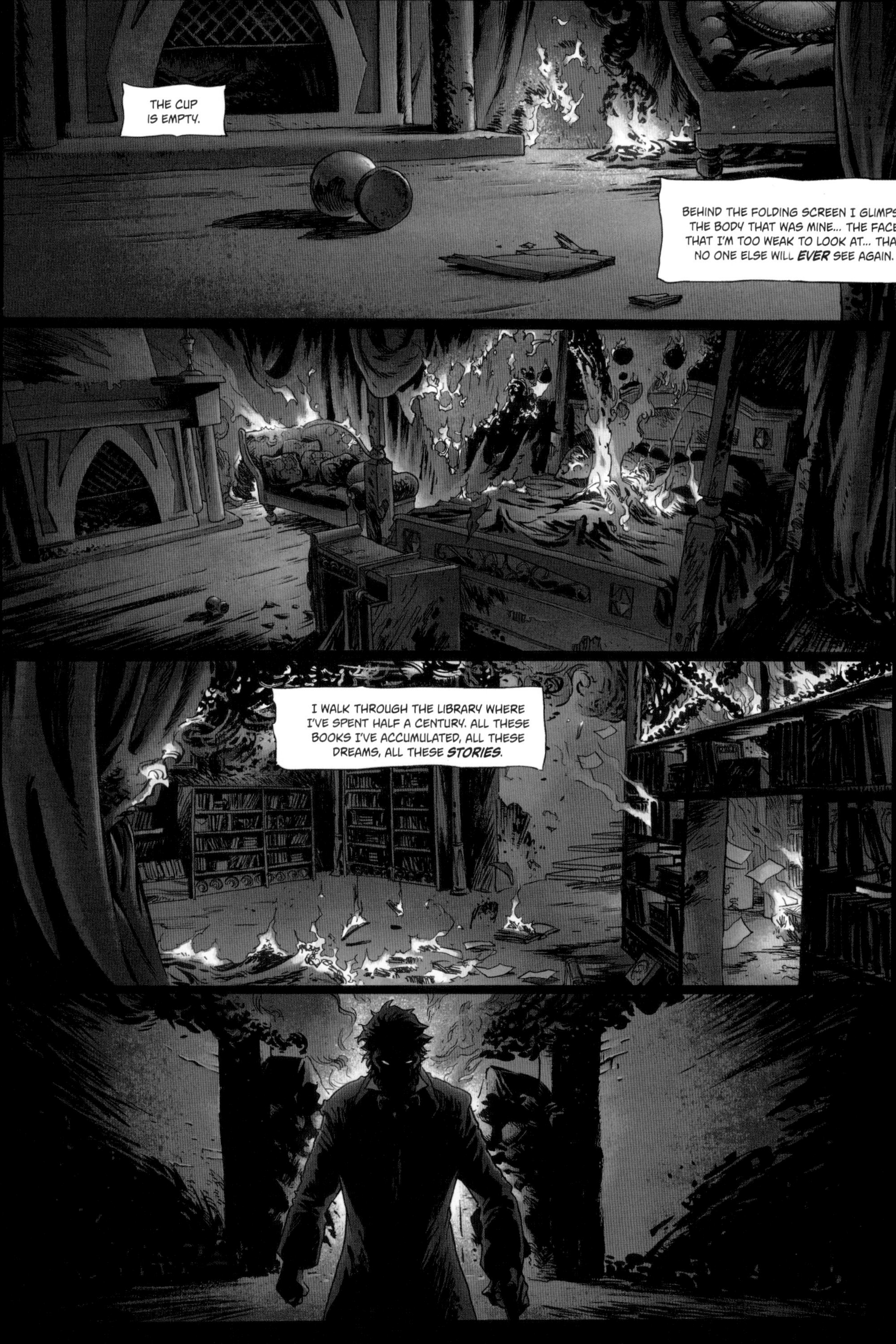
THE CUP IS EMPTY.
BEHIND THE FOLDING SCREEN I GLIMPSE THE BODY THAT WAS MINE... THE FACE THAT I'M TOO WEAK TO LOOK AT... THAT NO ONE ELSE WILL **EVER** SEE AGAIN.
I WALK THROUGH THE LIBRARY WHERE I'VE SPENT HALF A CENTURY. ALL THESE BOOKS I'VE ACCUMULATED, ALL THESE DREAMS, ALL THESE **STORIES**.

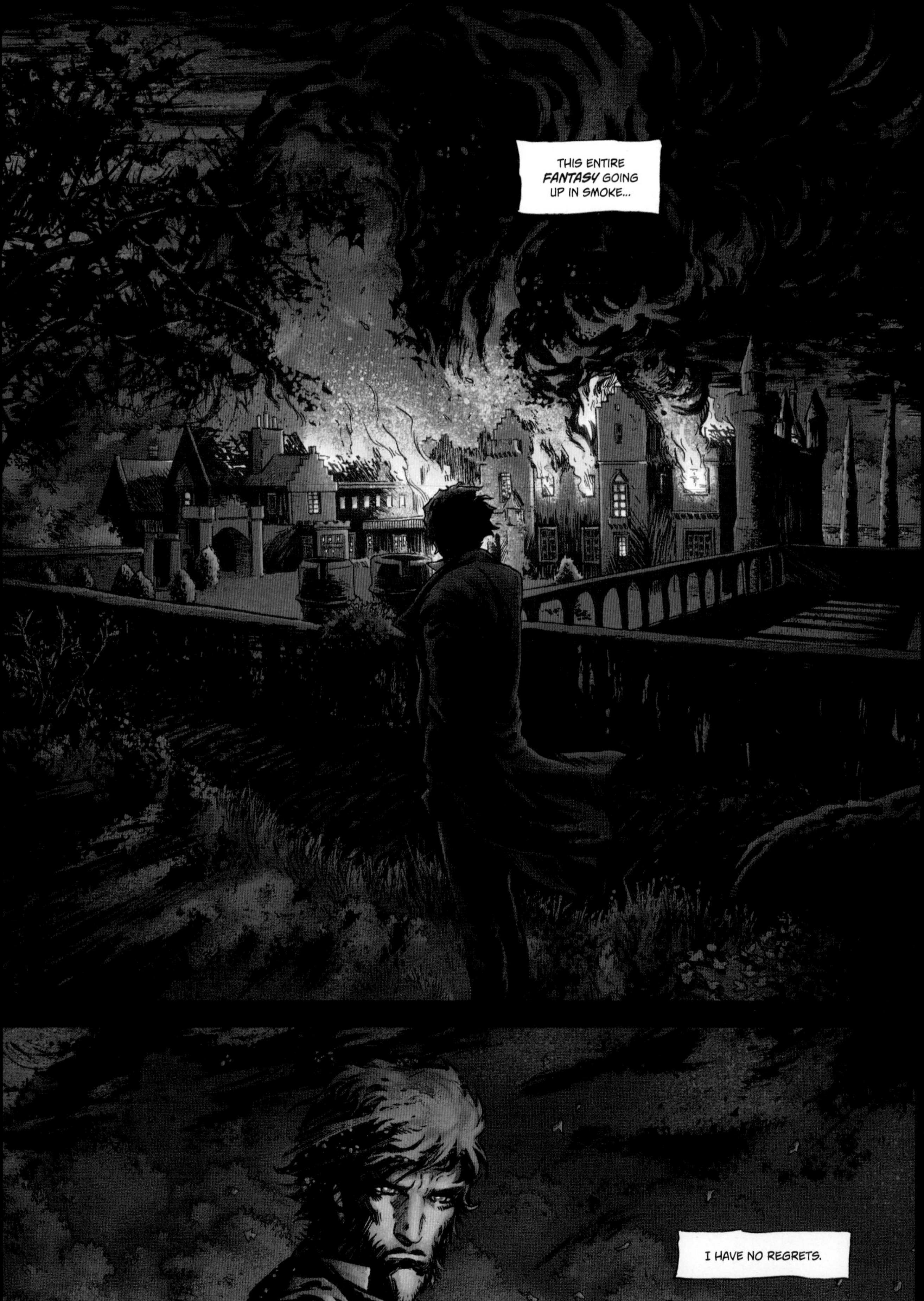
THIS ENTIRE FANTASY GOING UP IN SMOKE...
I HAVE NO REGRETS.

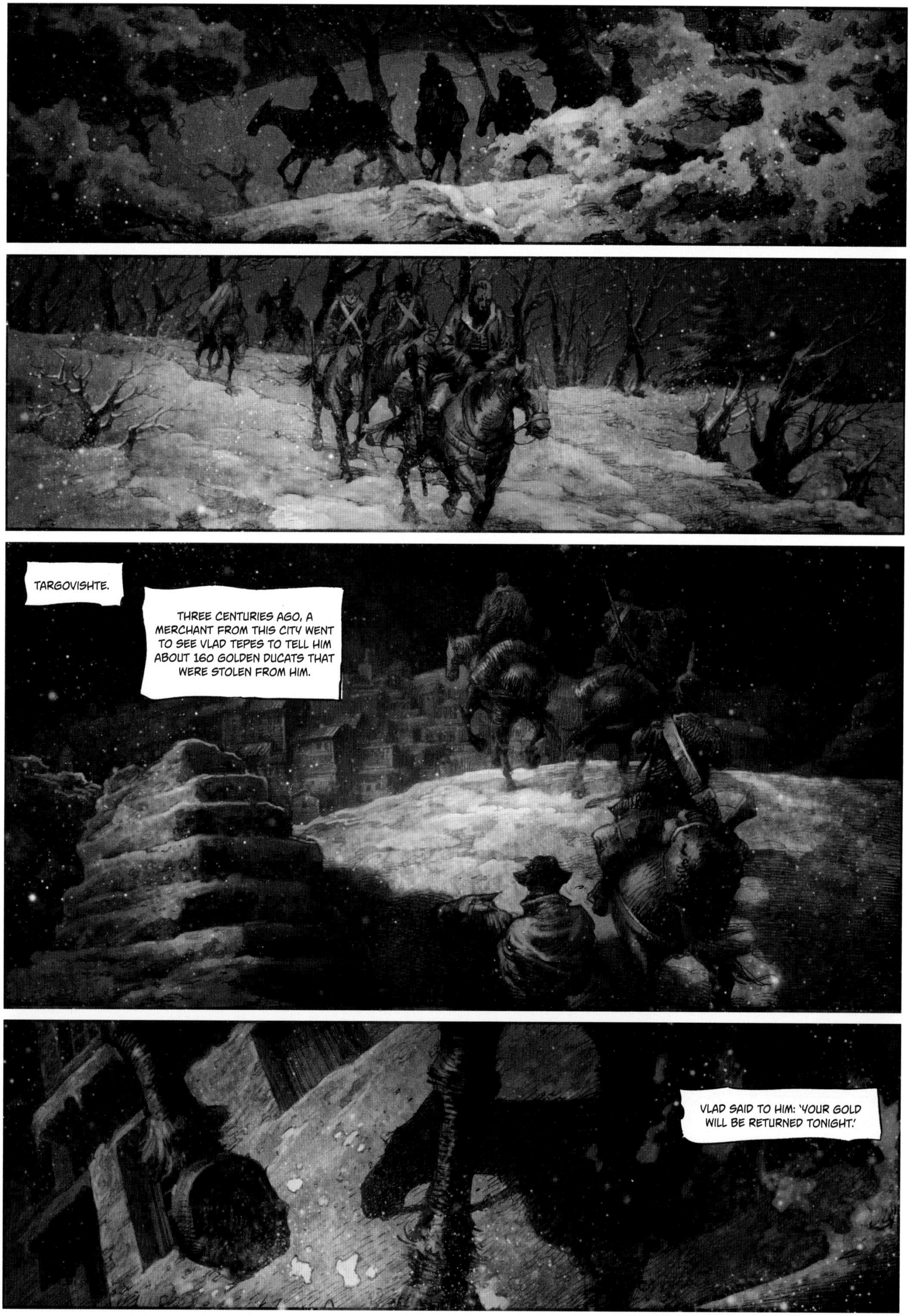
TARGOVISHTE.
THREE CENTURIES AGO, A MERCHANT FROM THIS CITY WENT TO SEE VLAD TEPES TO TELL HIM ABOUT 160 GOLDEN DUCATS THAT WERE STOLEN FROM HIM.
VLAD SAID TO HIM: 'YOUR GOLD WILL BE RETURNED TONIGHT.'

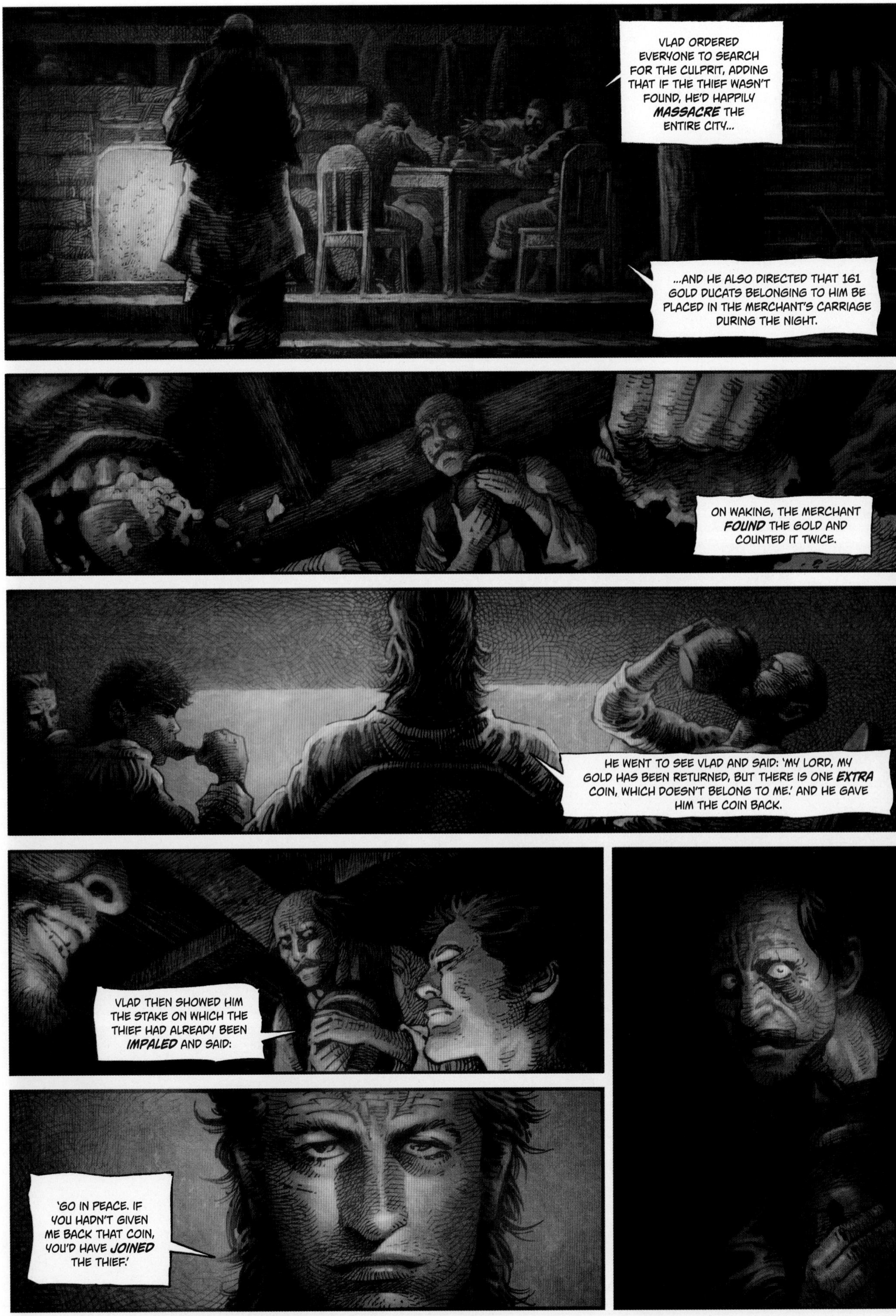
VLAD ORDERED EVERYONE TO SEARCH FOR THE CULPRIT, ADDING THAT IF THE THIEF WASN'T FOUND, HE'D HAPPILY MASSACRE THE ENTIRE CITY...
...AND HE ALSO DIRECTED THAT 161 GOLD DUCATS BELONGING TO HIM BE PLACED IN THE MERCHANT'S CARRIAGE DURING THE NIGHT.
ON WAKING, THE MERCHANT FOUND THE GOLD AND COUNTED IT TWICE.
HE WENT TO SEE VLAD AND SAID: 'MY LORD, MY GOLD HAS BEEN RETURNED, BUT THERE IS ONE EXTRA COIN, WHICH DOESN'T BELONG TO ME.' AND HE GAVE HIM THE COIN BACK.
VLAD THEN SHOWED HIM THE STAKE ON WHICH THE THIEF HAD ALREADY BEEN IMPALED AND SAID:
'GO IN PEACE. IF YOU HADN'T GIVEN ME BACK THAT COIN, YOU'D HAVE JOINED THE THIEF.'

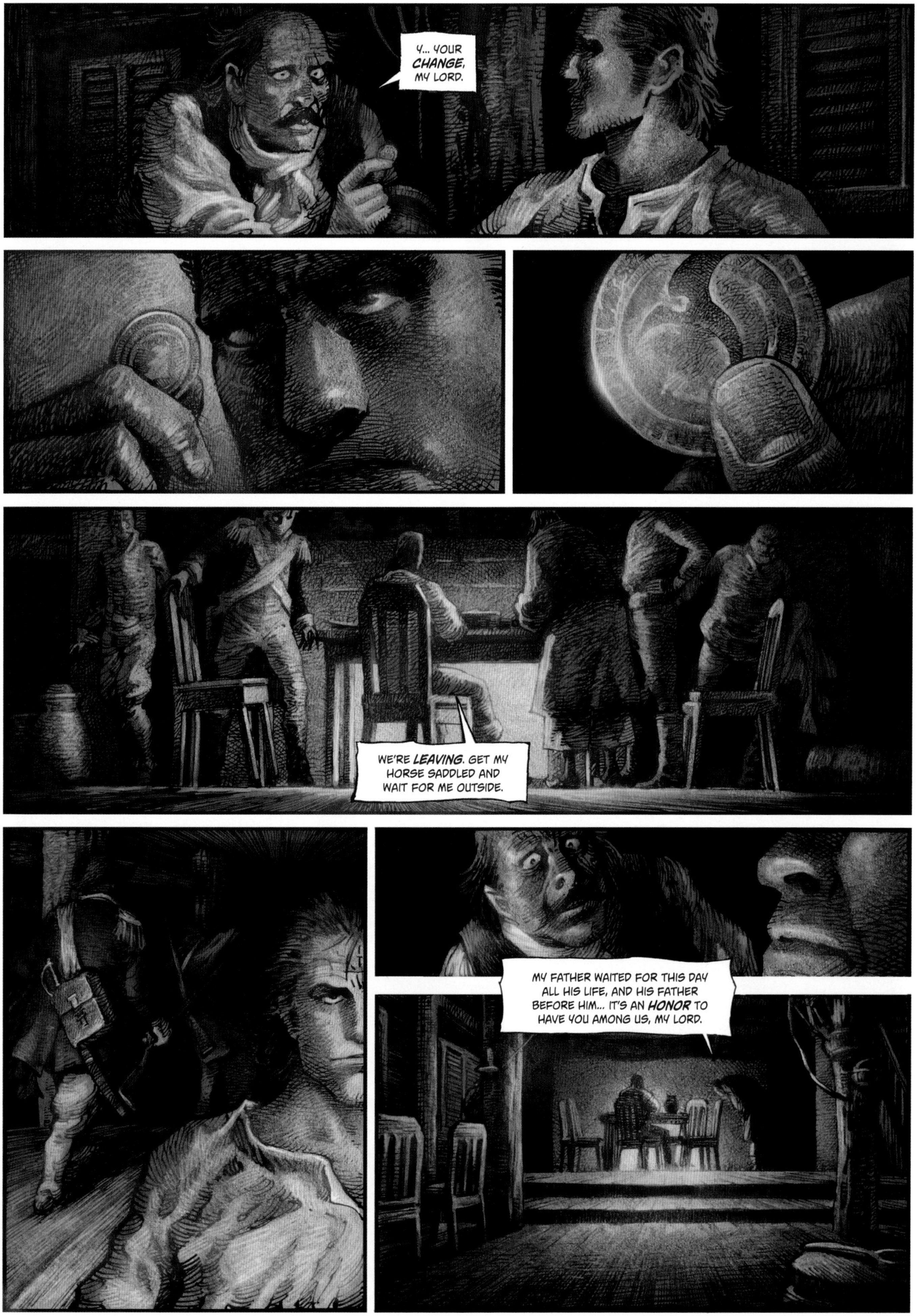
Y... YOUR CHANGE, MY LORD.
WE'RE LEAVING. GET MY HORSE SADDLED AND WAIT FOR ME OUTSIDE.
MY FATHER WAITED FOR THIS DAY ALL HIS LIFE, AND HIS FATHER BEFORE HIM... IT'S AN HONOR TO HAVE YOU AMONG US, MY LORD.

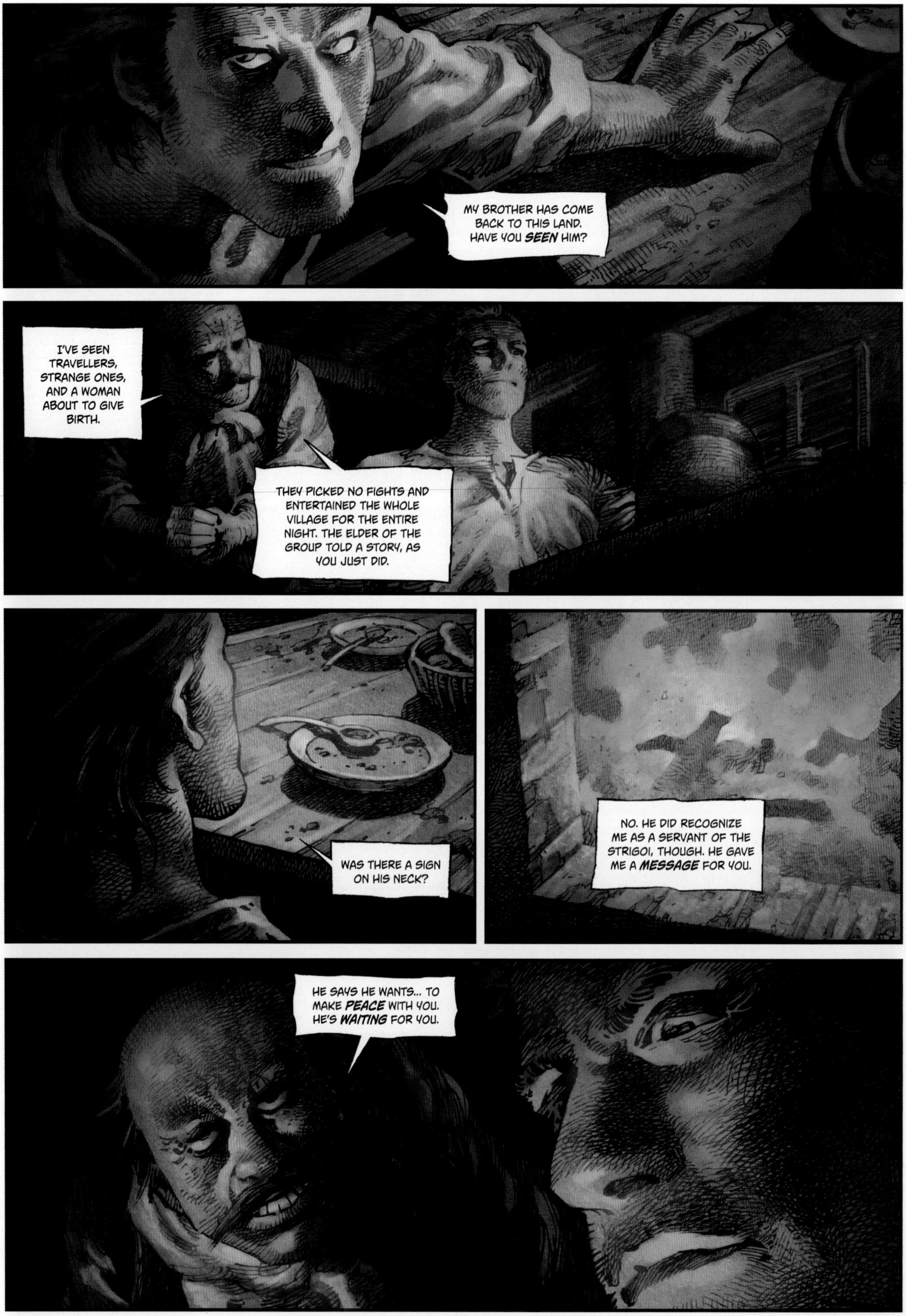
MY BROTHER HAS COME BACK TO THIS LAND. HAVE YOU SEEN HIM?
I'VE SEEN TRAVELLERS, STRANGE ONES, AND A WOMAN ABOUT TO GIVE BIRTH.
THEY PICKED NO FIGHTS AND ENTERTAINED THE WHOLE VILLAGE FOR THE ENTIRE NIGHT. THE ELDER OF THE GROUP TOLD A STORY, AS YOU JUST DID.
WAS THERE A SIGN ON HIS NECK?
NO. HE DID RECOGNIZE ME AS A SERVANT OF THE STRIGOI, THOUGH. HE GAVE ME A MESSAGE FOR YOU.
HE SAYS HE WANTS... TO MAKE PEACE WITH YOU. HE'S WAITING FOR YOU.

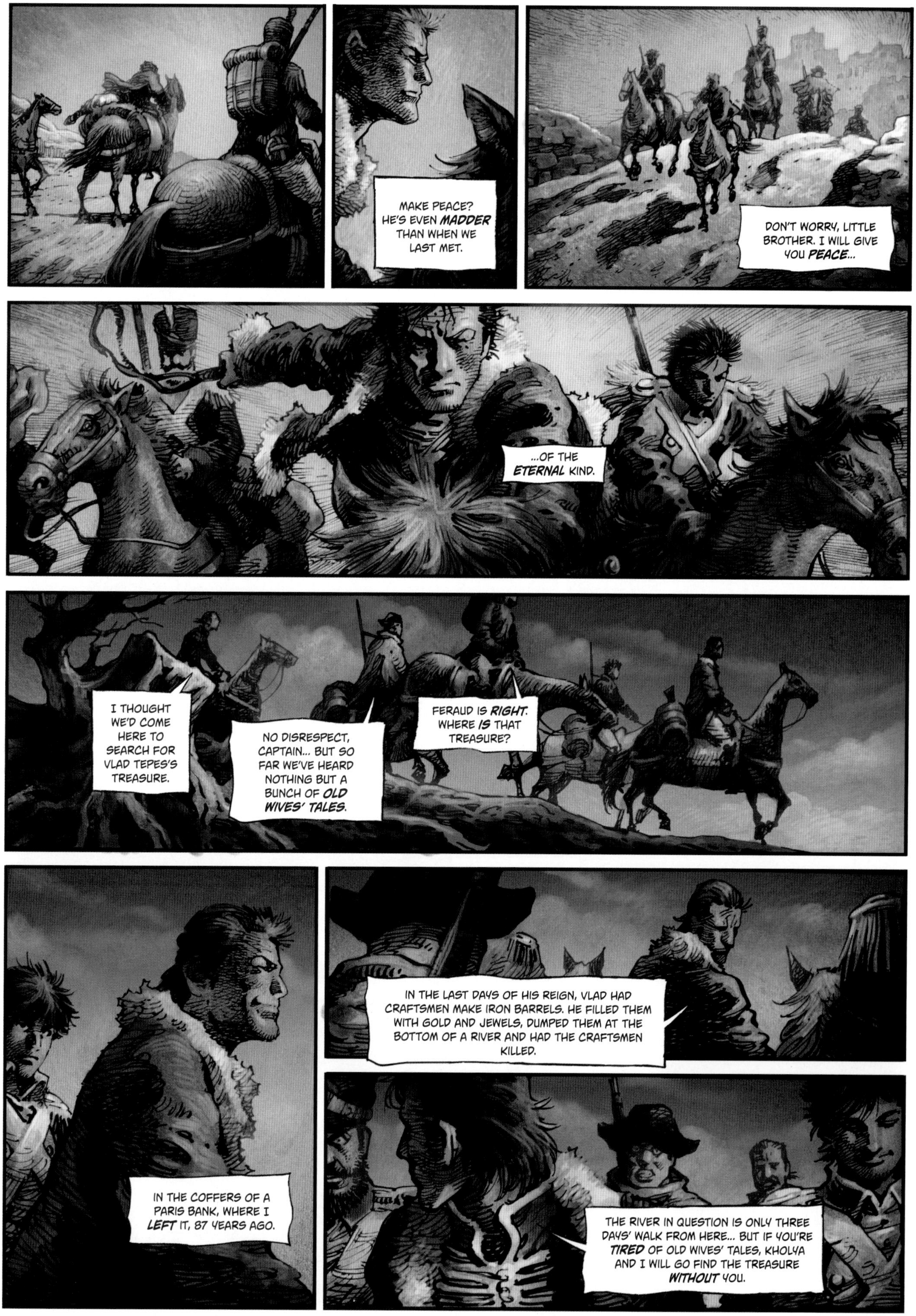
MAKE PEACE? HE'S EVEN MADDER THAN WHEN WE LAST MET.
DON'T WORRY, LITTLE BROTHER. I WILL GIVE YOU PEACE...
...OF THE ETERNAL KIND.
I THOUGHT WE'D COME HERE TO SEARCH FOR VLAD TEPES'S TREASURE.
NO DISRESPECT, CAPTAIN... BUT SO FAR WE'VE HEARD NOTHING BUT A BUNCH OF OLD WIVES' TALES.
FERAUD IS RIGHT. WHERE IS THAT TREASURE?
IN THE COFFERS OF A PARIS BANK, WHERE I LEFT IT, 87 YEARS AGO.
IN THE LAST DAYS OF HIS REIGN, VLAD HAD CRAFTSMEN MAKE IRON BARRELS. HE FILLED THEM WITH GOLD AND JEWELS, DUMPED THEM AT THE BOTTOM OF A RIVER AND HAD THE CRAFTSMEN KILLED.
THE RIVER IN QUESTION IS ONLY THREE DAYS' WALK FROM HERE... BUT IF YOU'RE TIRED OF OLD WIVES' TALES, KHOLYA AND I WILL GO FIND THE TREASURE WITHOUT YOU.

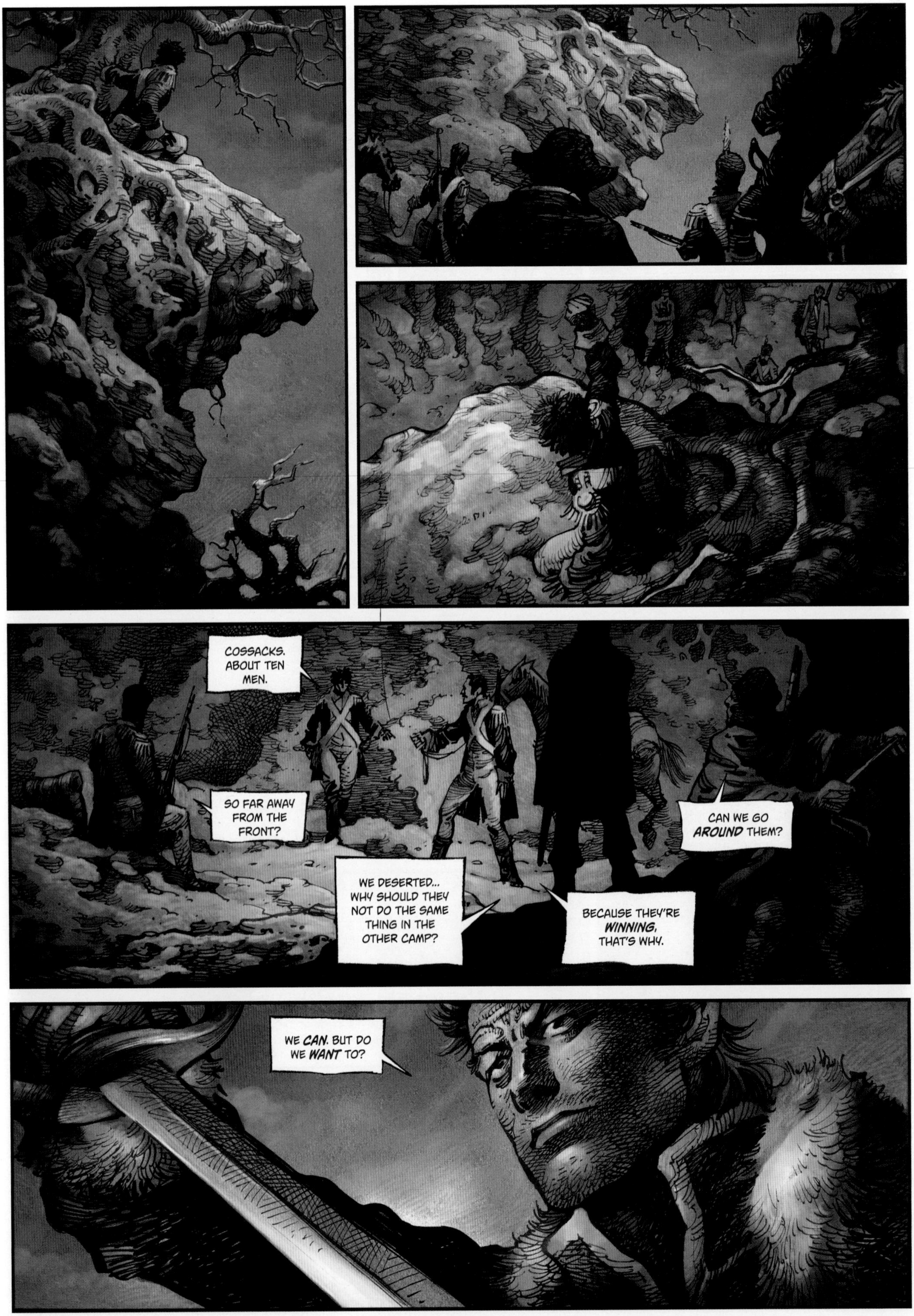
COSSACKS. ABOUT TEN MEN.
SO FAR AWAY FROM THE FRONT?
WE DESERTED... WHY SHOULD THEY NOT DO THE SAME THING IN THE OTHER CAMP?
BECAUSE THEY'RE WINNING, THAT'S WHY.
CAN WE GO AROUND THEM?
WE CAN. BUT DO WE WANT TO?

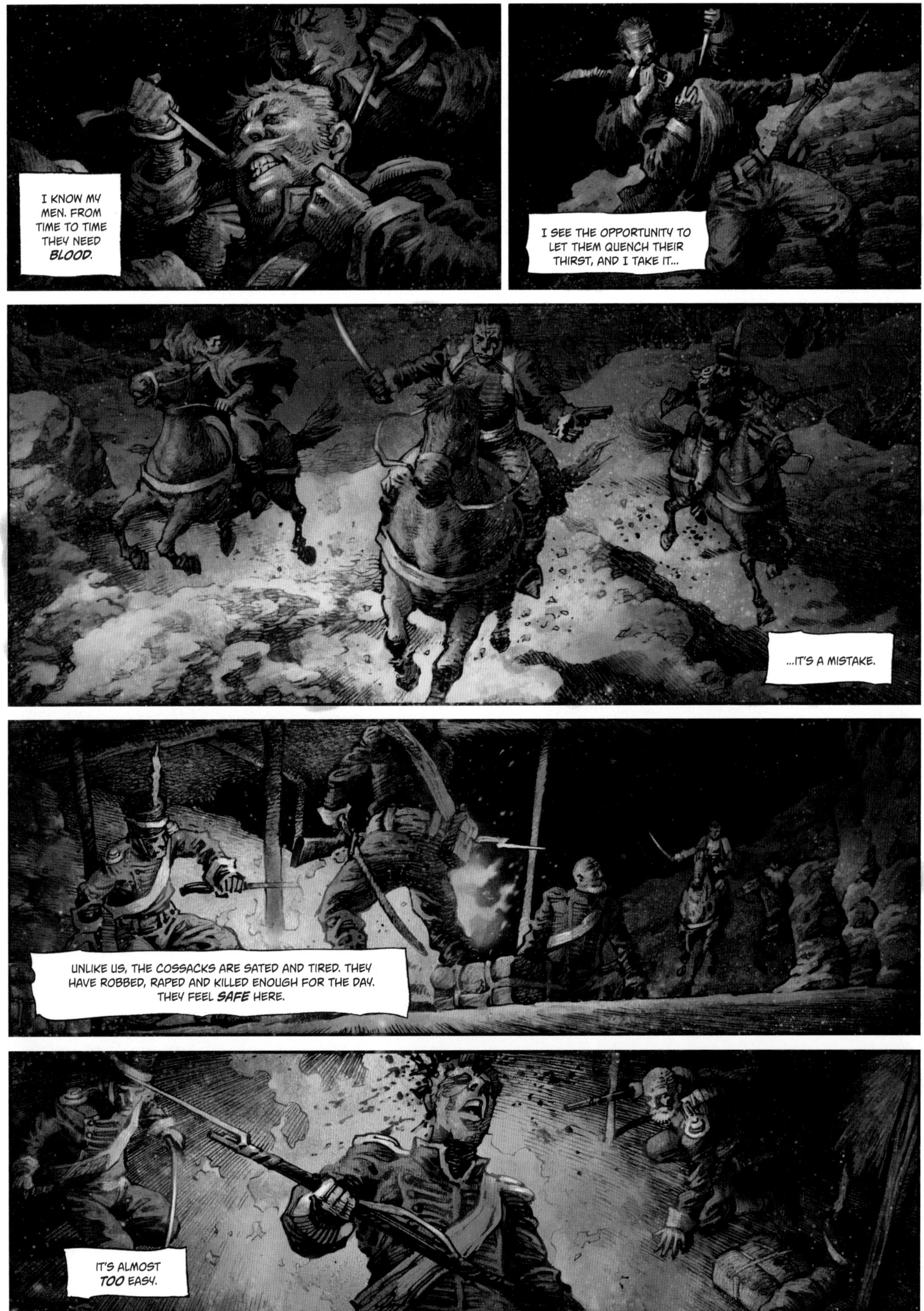
I KNOW MY MEN. FROM TIME TO TIME THEY NEED BLOOD.
I SEE THE OPPORTUNITY TO LET THEM QUENCH THEIR THIRST, AND I TAKE IT...
...IT'S A MISTAKE.
UNLIKE US, THE COSSACKS ARE SATED AND TIRED. THEY HAVE ROBBED, RAPED AND KILLED ENOUGH FOR THE DAY. THEY FEEL SAFE HERE.
IT'S ALMOST TOO EASY.

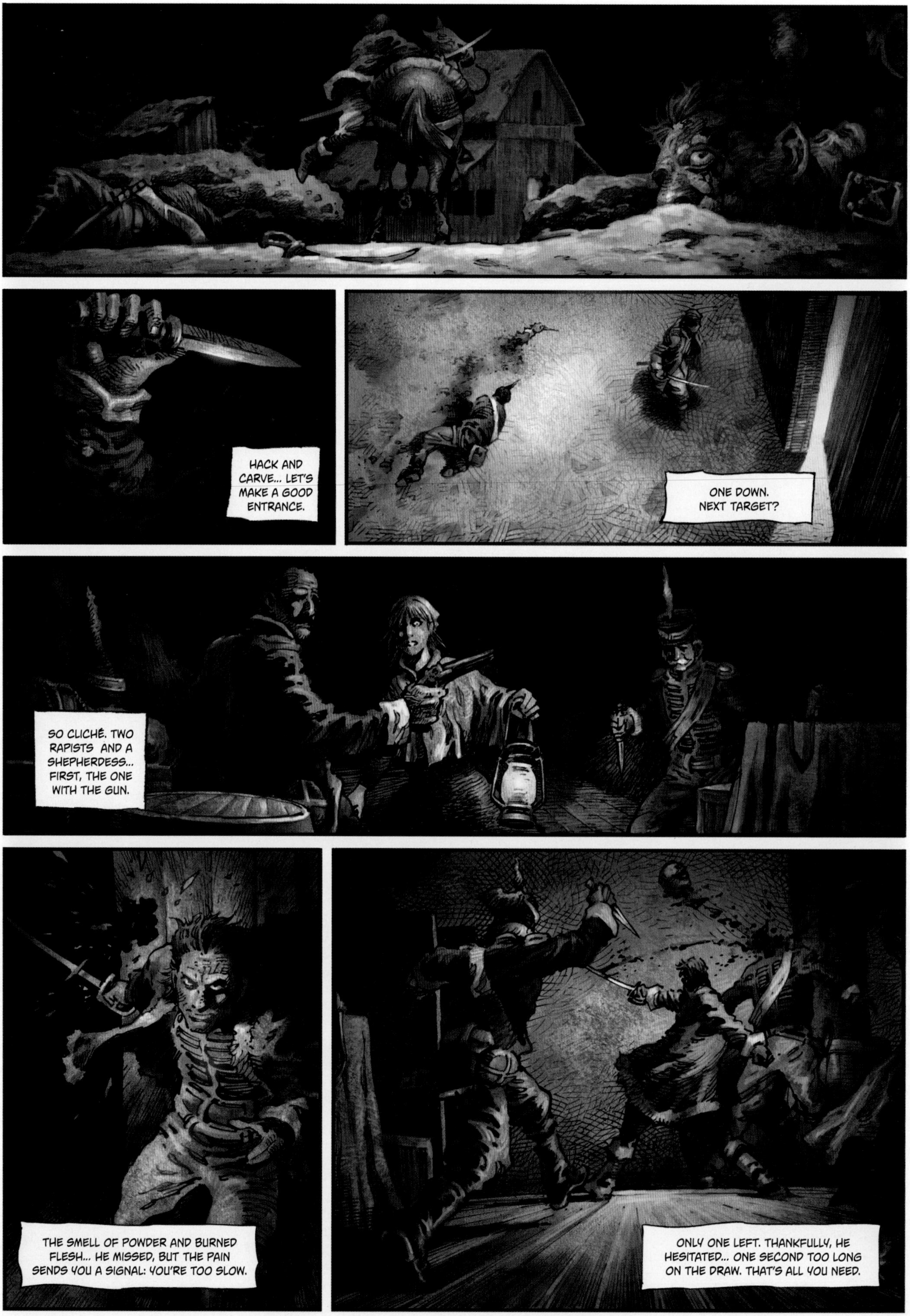
HACK AND CARVE... LET'S MAKE A GOOD ENTRANCE.
ONE DOWN. NEXT TARGET?
SO CLICHÉ. TWO RAPISTS AND A SHEPHERDESS... FIRST, THE ONE WITH THE GUN.
THE SMELL OF POWDER AND BURNED FLESH... HE MISSED, BUT THE PAIN SENDS YOU A SIGNAL: YOU'RE TOO SLOW.
ONLY ONE LEFT. THANKFULLY, HE HESITATED... ONE SECOND TOO LONG ON THE DRAW. THAT'S ALL YOU NEED.

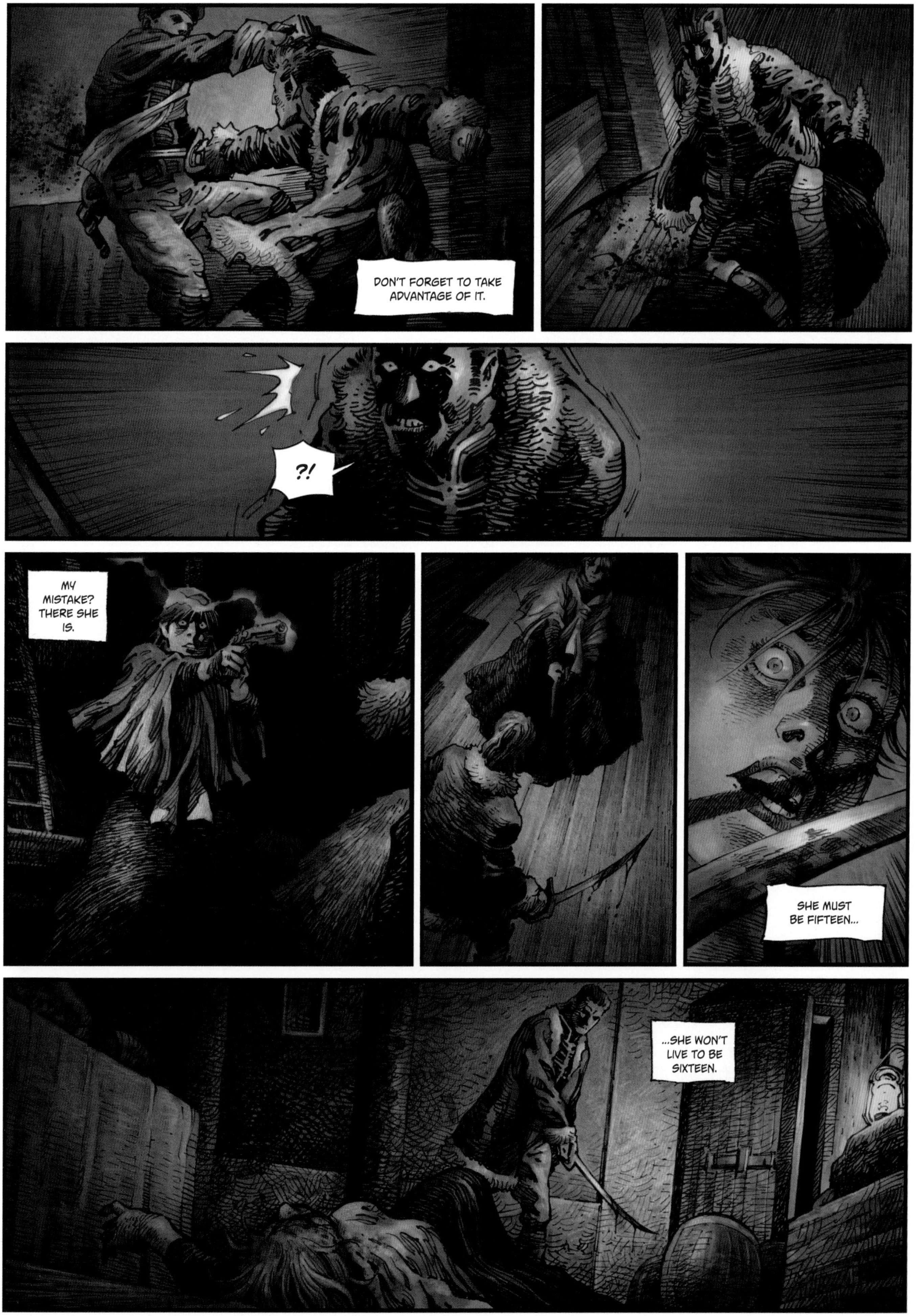

DON'T FORGET TO TAKE ADVANTAGE OF IT.
?!
MY MISTAKE? THERE SHE IS.
SHE MUST BE FIFTEEN...
...SHE WON'T LIVE TO BE SIXTEEN.

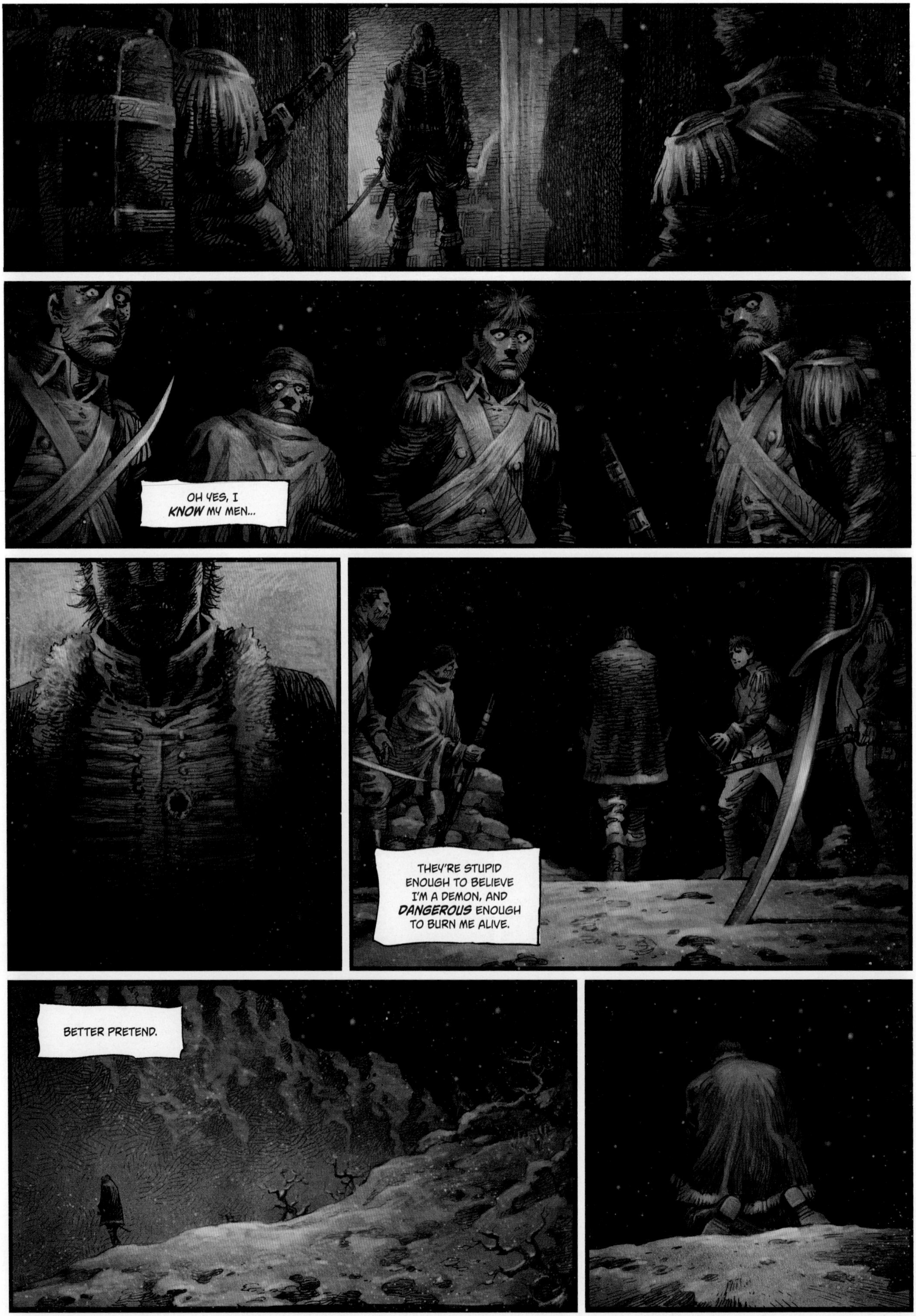
OH YES, I KNOW MY MEN...
THEY'RE STUPID ENOUGH TO BELIEVE I'M A DEMON, AND DANGEROUS ENOUGH TO BURN ME ALIVE.
BETTER PRETEND.

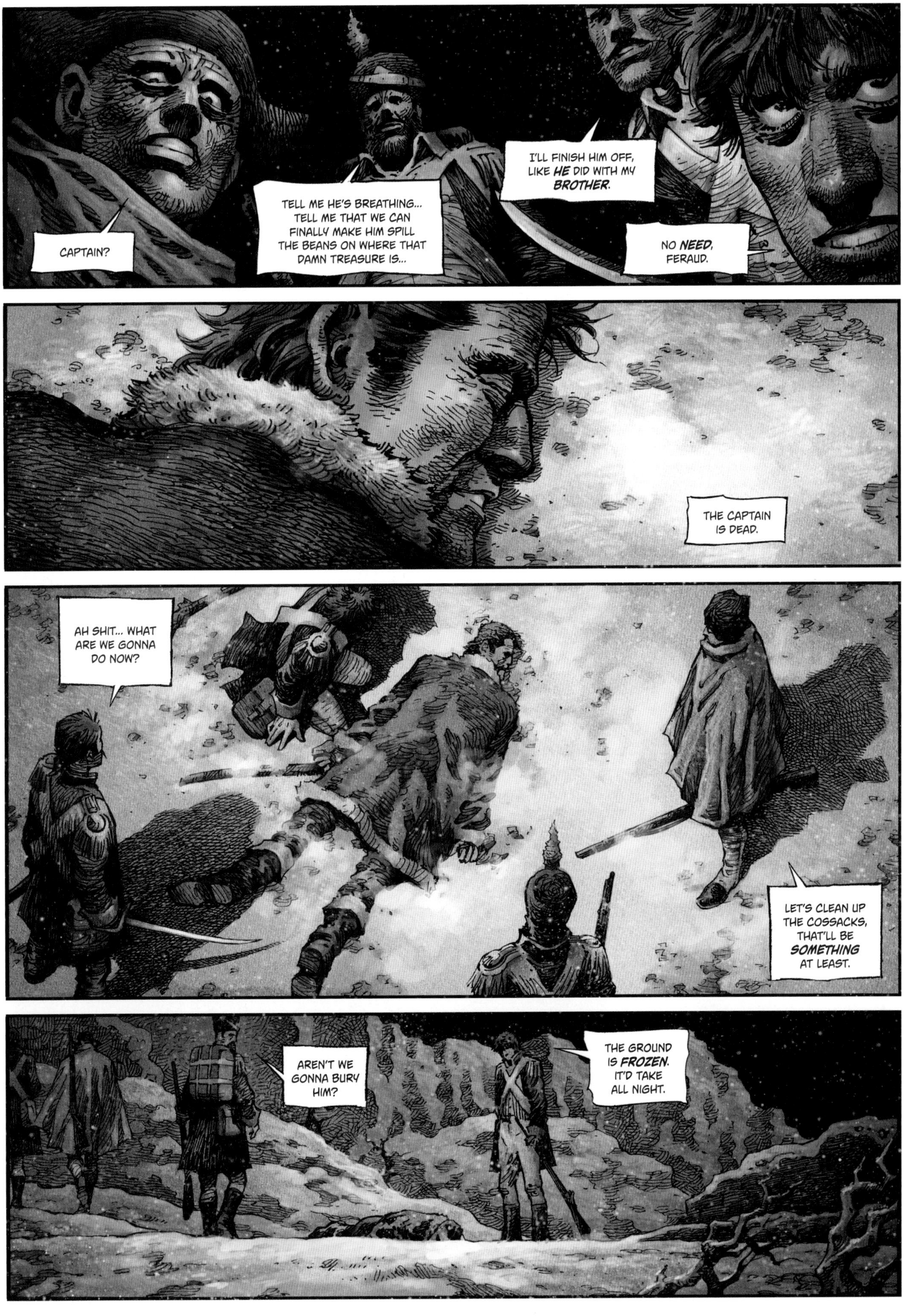
CAPTAIN?
TELL ME HE'S BREATHING... TELL ME THAT WE CAN FINALLY MAKE HIM SPILL THE BEANS ON WHERE THAT DAMN TREASURE IS...
I'LL FINISH HIM OFF, LIKE HE DID WITH MY BROTHER.
NO NEED, FERAUD.
THE CAPTAIN IS DEAD.
AH SHIT... WHAT ARE WE GONNA DO NOW?
LET'S CLEAN UP THE COSSACKS, THAT'LL BE SOMETHING AT LEAST.
AREN'T WE GONNA BURY HIM?
THE GROUND IS FROZEN. IT'D TAKE ALL NIGHT.

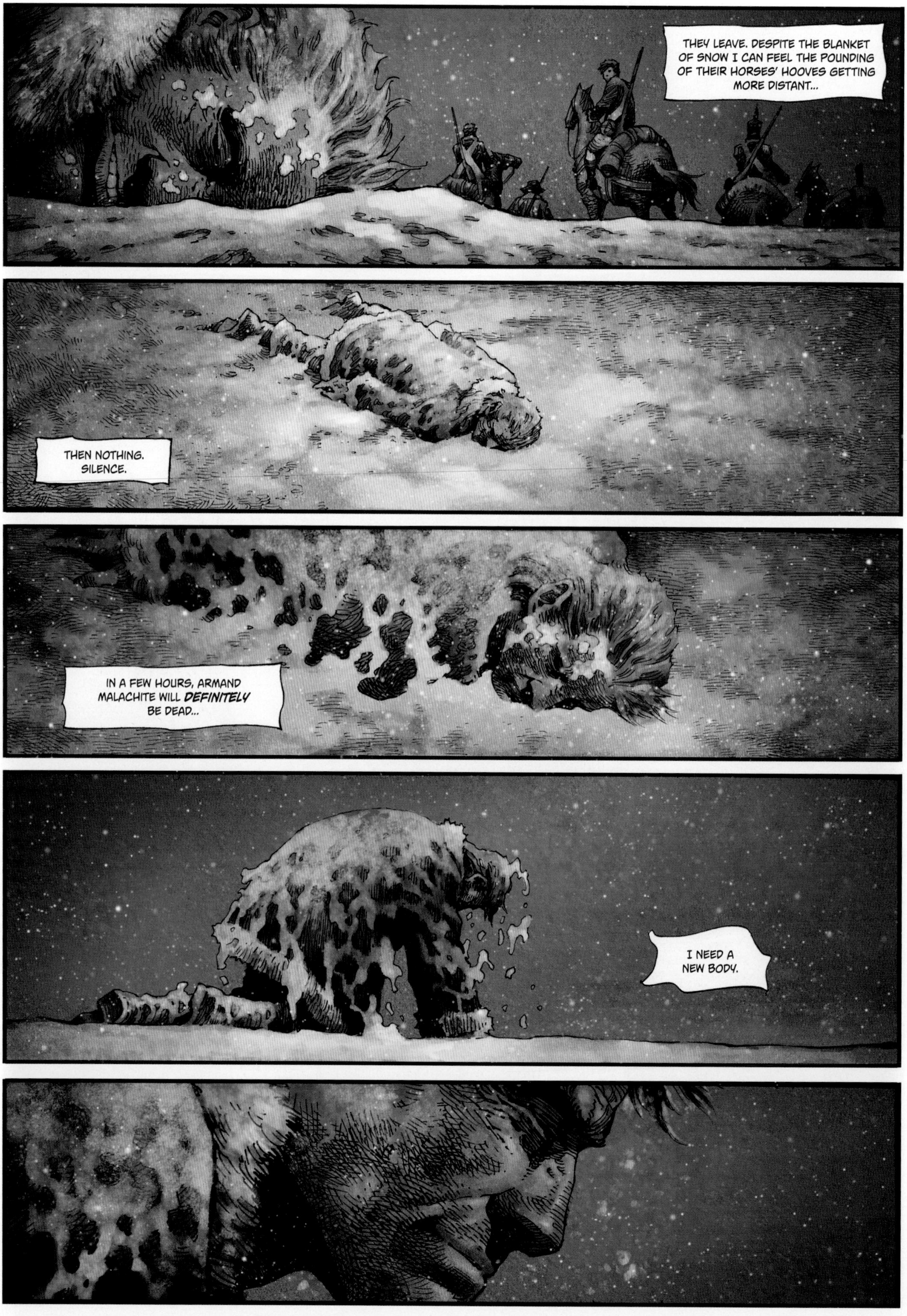
THEY LEAVE. DESPITE THE BLANKET OF SNOW I CAN FEEL THE POUNDING OF THEIR HORSES' HOOVES GETTING MORE DISTANT...
THEN NOTHING. SILENCE.
IN A FEW HOURS, ARMAND MALACHITE WILL DEFINITELY BE DEAD...
I NEED A NEW BODY.

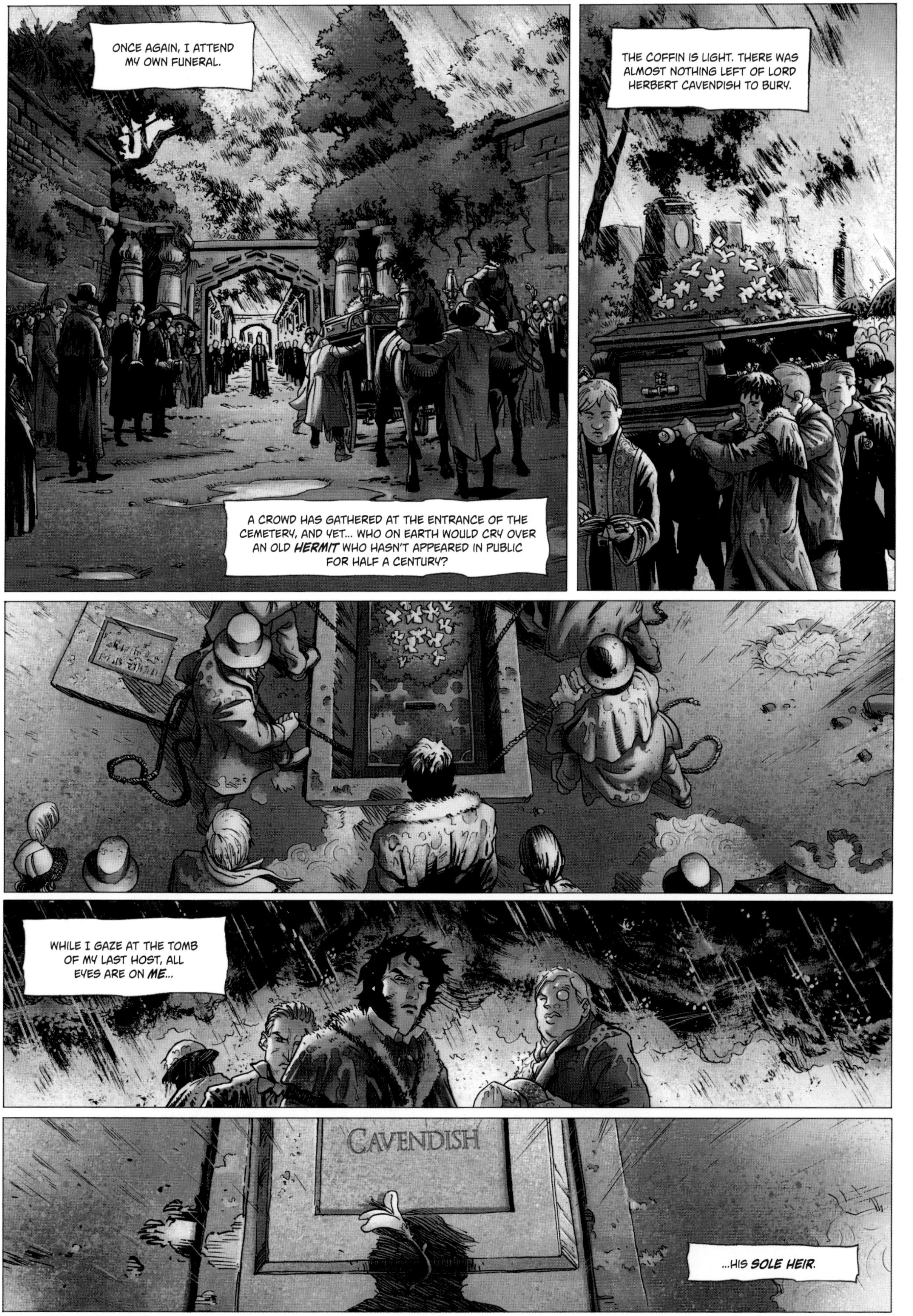
ONCE AGAIN, I ATTEND MY OWN FUNERAL.
A CROWD HAS GATHERED AT THE ENTRANCE OF THE CEMETERY, AND YET... WHO ON EARTH WOULD CRY OVER AN OLD HERMIT WHO HASN'T APPEARED IN PUBLIC FOR HALF A CENTURY?
THE COFFIN IS LIGHT. THERE WAS ALMOST NOTHING LEFT OF LORD HERBERT CAVENDISH TO BURY.
WHILE I GAZE AT THE TOMB OF MY LAST HOST, ALL EYES ARE ON ME...
CAVENDISH
...HIS SOLE HEIR.

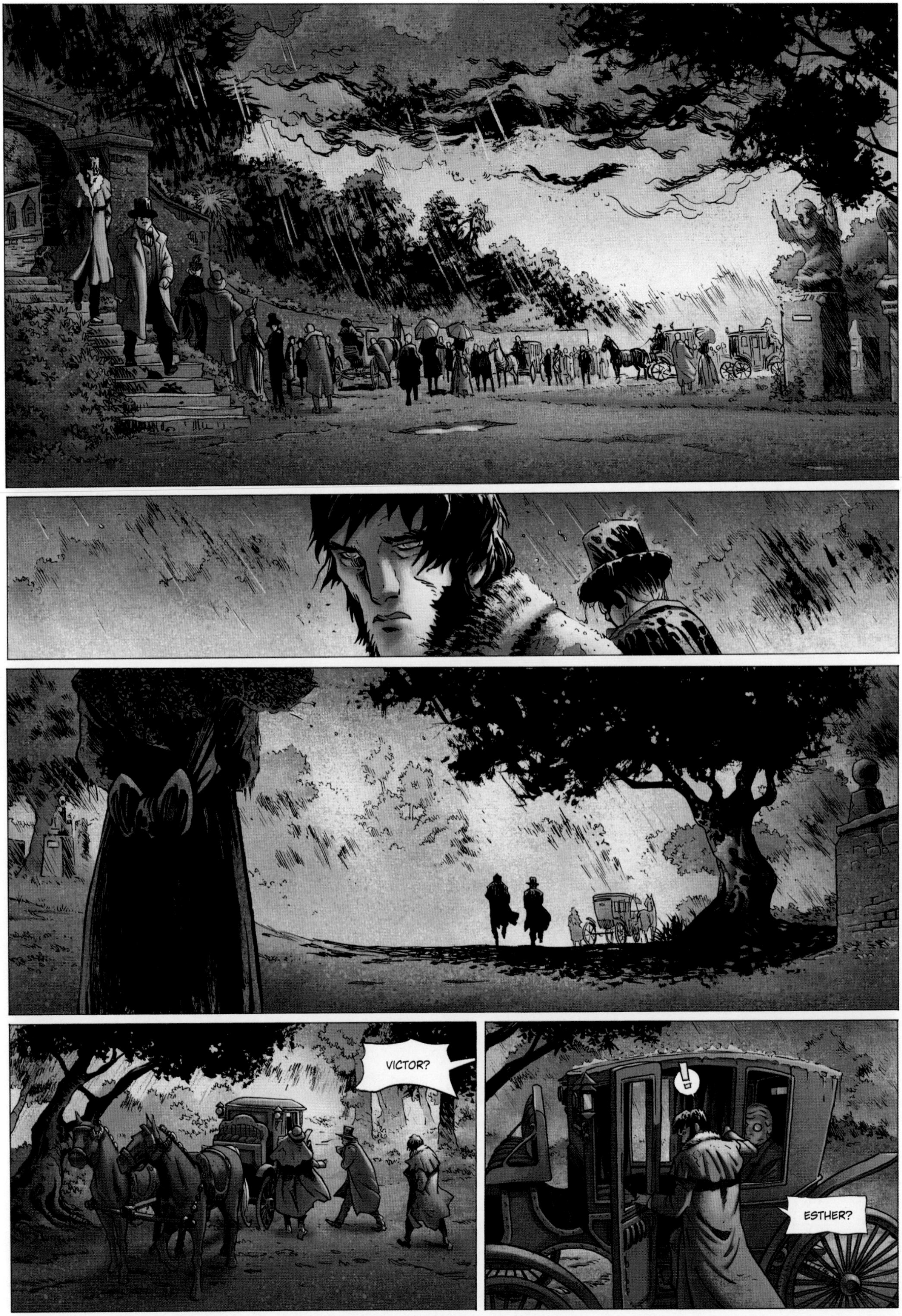
VICTOR?
ESTHER?

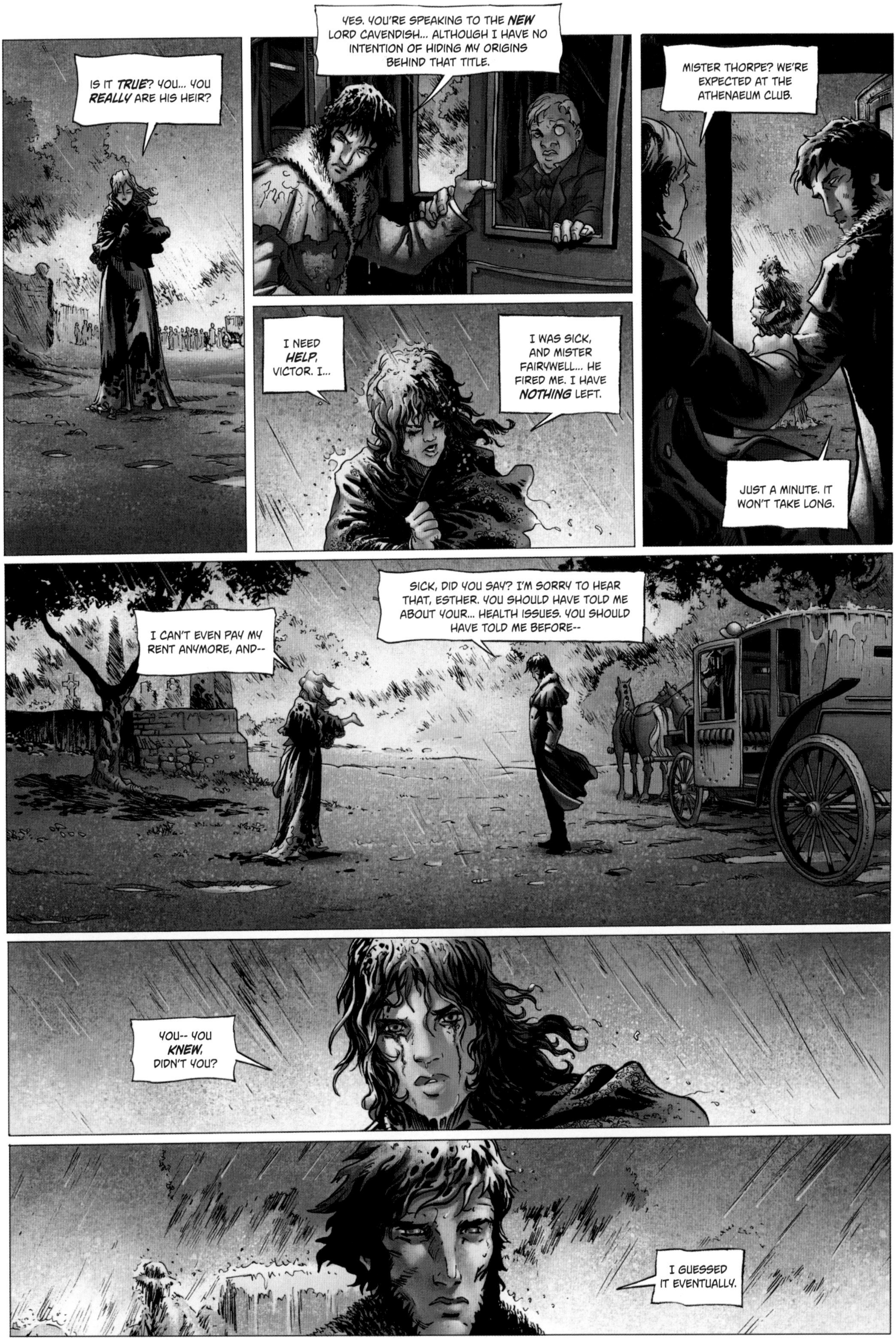
IS IT TRUE? YOU... YOU REALLY ARE HIS HEIR?
YES. YOU'RE SPEAKING TO THE NEW LORD CAVENDISH... ALTHOUGH I HAVE NO INTENTION OF HIDING MY ORIGINS BEHIND THAT TITLE.
MISTER THORPE? WE'RE EXPECTED AT THE ATHENAEUM CLUB.
I NEED HELP, VICTOR. I...
I WAS SICK, AND MISTER FAIRYWELL... HE FIRED ME. I HAVE NOTHING LEFT.
JUST A MINUTE. IT WON'T TAKE LONG.
I CAN'T EVEN PAY MY RENT ANYMORE, AND--
SICK, DID YOU SAY? I'M SORRY TO HEAR THAT, ESTHER. YOU SHOULD HAVE TOLD ME ABOUT YOUR... HEALTH ISSUES. YOU SHOULD HAVE TOLD ME BEFORE--
YOU-- YOU KNEW, DIDN'T YOU?
I GUESSED IT EVENTUALLY.

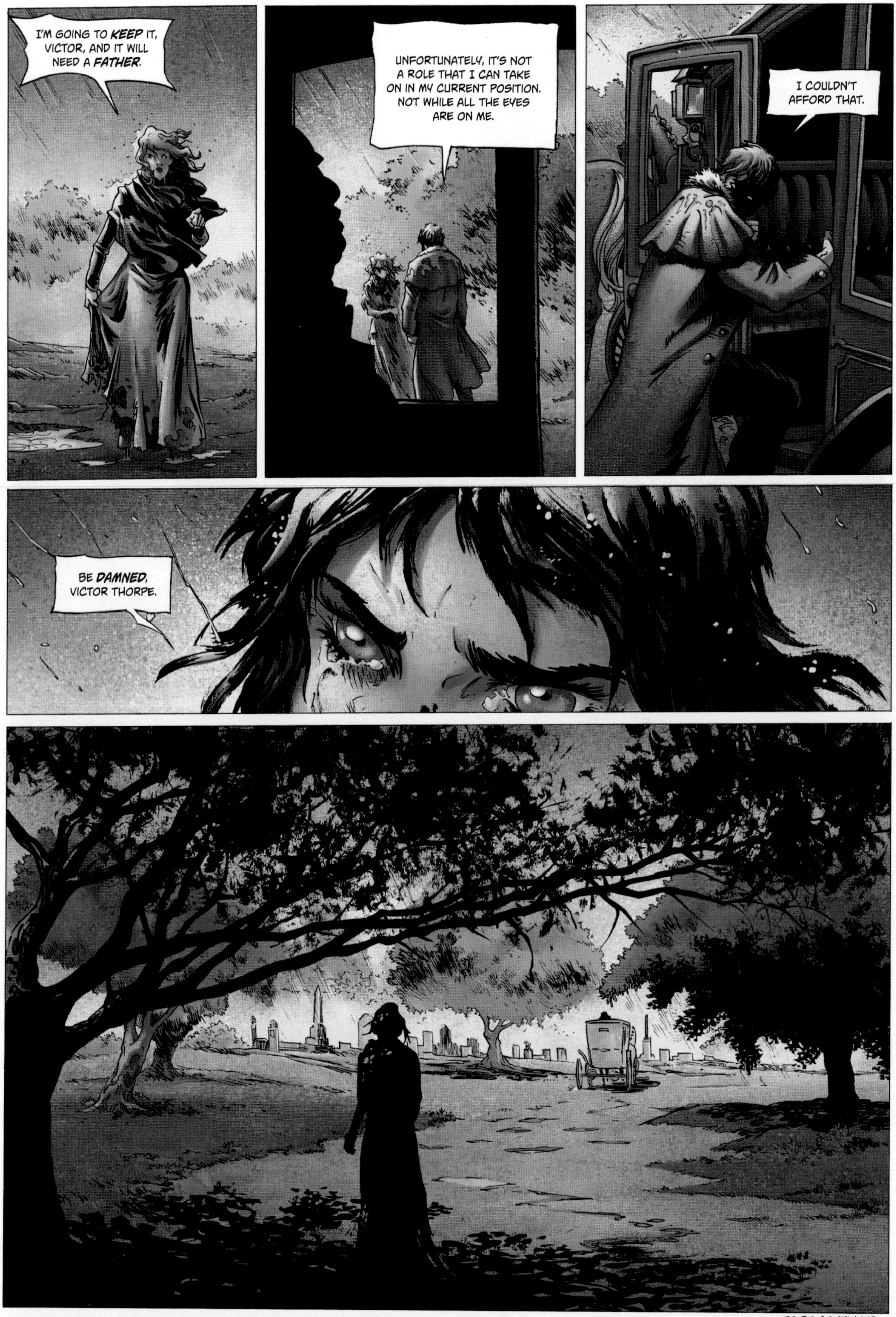
I'M GOING TO KEEP IT, VICTOR, AND IT WILL NEED A FATHER.
UNFORTUNATELY, IT'S NOT A ROLE THAT I CAN TAKE ON IN MY CURRENT POSITION. NOT WHILE ALL THE EYES ARE ON ME.
I COULDN'T AFFORD THAT.
BE DAMNED, VICTOR THORPE.

TO BE CONTINUED...